Reaching Muslims

Reaching
Muslims

A Christian's Guide to Islam

Mona Sabah

GETHSEMANE PRESS

GETHSEMANE PRESS

Reaching Muslims - A Christian's Guide to Islam

Copyright © 2018 by Mona Sabah Earnest

This title is also available as an eBook
ISBN-13: 978-0-9986378-1-5 (soft cover)

Library of Congress Control Number: **[LCCN]: 2018947900**
Published by GETHSEMANE PRESS
Edmond, Oklahoma

Cover Design: Original art by Mona Sabah & Designer Sarah Earnest

Inside Cover page art: Arabic Calligraphy of Bible Romans 3:23-4 common use

Icons and pictures used within the book are all available free of charge from creative
common use sites like wiki commons and all-silhouettes.com

Printed in the United States of America

A Great Multitude from Every Nation

After this I looked, and behold, a great multitude that no one could number, from every nation, from all tribes and peoples and languages, standing before the throne and before the Lamb, clothed in white robes, with palm branches in their hands, and crying out with a loud voice, "Salvation belongs to our God who sits on the throne, and to the Lamb!" And all the angels were standing around the throne and around the elders and the four living creatures, and they fell on their faces before the throne and worshiped God, saying, "Amen! Blessing and glory and wisdom and thanksgiving and honor and power and might be to our God forever and ever! Amen."

Revelation 7:9-12

To my children Jacob, Joshua and Sarah

AND

To my brothers and sisters in Christ Jesus. Thank you for being my family in Christ when I had none. May you love others the way Christ loves us.

CONTENTS

Mona's Testimony

Mona Sabah was born in the Middle East, and spent her younger years in Saudi Arabia, Kuwait, the UAE, Europe and Pakistan. At age 10, she and her family moved to the United States. At age 35, Mona read the chapter of the Quran about Isa Ibn Maryam, or Jesus, the son of Mary. She accepted Christ as her Savior when the Gospel was finally shared by a pastor at a local church and has made it her mission to speak about the cultural implications of Islam and Christianity to groups across the country. She openly shares her testimony on growing up Muslim in the US, exploring assumptions and beliefs about Islam and Christianity to stress the importance of sharing the Gospel. In February 2017, she published her first book "From Isa to Christ - A Muslim Woman's Search for the Hand of God." She is married and has three children.

Now who is there to harm you if you are zealous for what is good? But even if you should suffer for righteousness' sake, you will be blessed. Have no fear of them, nor be troubled, but in your hearts honor Christ the Lord as holy, always being prepared to make a defense to anyone who asks you for a reason for the hope that is in you; yet do it with gentleness and respect, having a good conscience, so that, when you are slandered, those who revile your good behavior in Christ may be put to shame. For it is better to suffer for doing good, if that should be God's will, than for doing evil.

1Peter 3:13-17

How to Use This Book

This book is meant to be used as a workbook to help summarize what you learn, to record ideas on how to initiate a conversation and how to invite a Muslim (or any other non-believer) into the family of Christ. There are many assumptions made by both Christians and Muslims, I hope to share nuances from my own life and previous beliefs that will help to bridge the Gospel to Muslims. My aim is to help the reader gain an understanding of not just the religion of Islam, but also the rich traditions, culture, other Islamic readings, teachings and places that can cause confusion, especially when translated from Arabic to English.

I personally appreciate it when authors use the entire passage of the Bible to make their claim. I would like to extend the same respect to Muslims by using complete passages of the Quran and the Hadith wherever possible. For this reason, you will see large sections from the Islamic writings in the book. It is also helpful to know what the passage says in its entirety to draw your own conclusion.

There are fill-in-the-blank questions at the end of each chapter that highlight important facts about Islam. The answer key, along with a glossary of frequently used terms are located in the appendix. I encourage you to not immediately flip to the back of the book but to take the time to do some research and find the answers. You might be surprised at all the things you will learn!

I have shared my testimony and taught about Islamic practices and beliefs over the last decade. This book is designed to answer the frequently asked questions I receive almost every time I speak and to compile these answers into one interactive guidebook. I hope you will find it to be useful to you.

Chapter 1

History of Islam

Thus says the LORD, the King of Israel
and his Redeemer, the LORD of hosts:
"I am the first and I am the last;
besides me there is no god.
Who is like me? Let him proclaim it.
Let him declare and set it before me,
since I appointed an ancient people.
Let them declare what is to come, and what will happen.
Fear not, nor be afraid;
have I not told you from of old and declared it?
And you are my witnesses!
Is there a God besides me?
There is no Rock; I know not any."
Isaiah 44:6-8

The Beginning

Islam begins with the affirmation of the statement that Allah is one and ends with the assertion that Muhammad is the last prophet. Muhammad (or also written as Mohammad 570 AD - 632 AD) is known to Muslims as the "seal of the prophets" and the founder of Islam. He was born in 570 AD, was orphaned at a young age and then raised by his paternal uncle Abu Talib. His family descended from the merchant clan of Banu Hashim and he followed in their footsteps in trade. He married Khadija (or Khadeejah), his first wife when he was 25 and she was 40 years old. She was considered to be a great catch, since she was widowed and was running her deceased husband's business. She had hired Muhammad to negotiate a few business deals for her and thus earned his complete trust.

At that time, most of Arabia worshipped idols. It was a common pagan practice to retreat to caves in Arabia to meditate. On one of these spiritual retreats, Muhammad claimed he was visited by an angel of light (or a demon- he was not sure) in Cave Hira around 610 AD and received a revelation. He was 40 years old at that time.

Quran, Hadith & Sira

Some terms to know when studying Islam are Quran, Hadith and Sira. Muslims believe that the Quran is the fourth and final revelation of Allah through his prophet, Muhammad. The book must be read in Arabic, as Islam considers that to be the language of Heaven There is no passage in the Quran or the Hadith that make this claim, yet all prayers also are mandatory to be done in Arabic.

Quran means "to recite" and contains faithfully recorded recitations that Muhammad received from the angel Gabriel. Muhammad was considered to be illiterate, yet the angel told him to read. Everything he said while covered under a blanket during a revelation was the Quran. Anything he said afterwards to explain the verses became the Hadith. The Hadith is a collection of the traditions of Muhammad and there are six writers of the Hadith, with Sahih Bukhari being one from which many Muslims quote. Sahih Bukhari has nine volumes with over 4000 Hadith (many repeat, so can count them to be anywhere from 2000-4000) while the second most quoted Hadith Sahih Muslim has around 2000 Hadith[1]. Some are considered to be strong and others weak (not much support for them). The word "Sahih[2]" means authentic, valid or sound in Arabic.

The following excerpt is from the Hadith and the Sira about the sequence of events that started his legacy as the prophet of Islam.
****

From the Hadith and Sira of the Prophet:

It is reported in *al-Saheehayn* from 'Urwah ibn al-Zubayr that 'Aa'ishah the wife of the Prophet said:
"The beginning of the Revelation that came to the Messenger of Allah was good dreams; he never saw a dream but it came true like bright daylight. Then seclusion was made dear to him, and he used to go to the cave of Hiraa' and worship there, which means that he went and devoted himself to worship for a number of nights before coming back to his family to collect more provisions, then he would go back again. Then he would go back to Khadeejah to collect more provisions. (This went on) until the truth came to him suddenly when he was in the cave of Hiraa'. The angel came and said, 'Read!' The Messenger of Allah said, 'I am not a reader.' He said, Then he took hold of me and squeezed me until I could not bear it any more then he released me and said, 'Read!' I said, 'I am not a reader.' He took hold of me and squeezed me a second time until I could not

---

[1] Hadith of Prophet Muhammad at your Fingertips. https://www.sunnah.com/
[2] An Introduction To The Science Of Hadith
https://www.islamic-awareness.org/hadith/ulum/asb7.html

bear it any more, then he released me and said, 'Read!' I said, 'I am not a reader.' He took hold of me and squeezed me a third time until I could not bear it any more, then he released me and said,

'Read! In the Name of your Lord Who has created (all that exists).
He has created man from a clot (a piece of thick coagulated blood).
Read! And your Lord is the Most Generous.
Who has taught (the writing) by the pen.
He has taught man that which he knew not.'
[Surah al-'Alaq 96:1-5 – interpretation of the meaning]

Then the Messenger of Allah went back with his heart beating wildly, until he came to Khadeejah and said, 'Cover me! Cover me!' They covered him till his fear went away. Then he said to Khadeejah, 'O Khadeejah, I fear for myself,' and he told her what had happened. Khadeejah said, 'Nay, be of good cheer, for by Allah, Allah will never disgrace you. You uphold the ties of kinship, speak truthfully, help the poor and destitute, serve your guests generously and assist those who are stricken by calamity.'

Then Khadeejah took him to Waraqah ibn Nawfal, the son of her paternal uncle. He was a man who had become a Christian during the jaahiliyyah. He used to write Arabic script and he used to write from the Gospel in Arabic as much as Allah willed he should write. He was an old man who had become blind. Khadeejah said, 'O son of my uncle, listen to what your nephew says.' Waraqah said: 'O son of my brother, what have you seen?' [The Prophet] told him what he had seen. Waraqah said: 'This is the Naamoos [Jibreel] who came down to Musa. Would that I were young and could live until the time when your people will drive you out.'

The Messenger of Allah said, 'Will they really drive me out?' Waraqah said, 'Yes. Never has there come a man with that which you have brought, but he was persecuted. If I should live to see that day, I will support you strongly.' But a few days later, Waraqah died, and the Revelation also ceased for a while, until the Messenger of Allah was filled with grief.

Muhammad ibn Shihaab said: Abu Salamah ibn 'Abd al-Rahmaan told me that Jaabir ibn 'Abd-Allaah al-Ansaari said: "The Messenger of Allah said, speaking of that period when the revelation ceased: 'Whilst I was walking, I heard a voice from the sky. I looked up and saw the angel who had come to me in Hiraa', sitting on a chair between the heavens and the earth. I felt scared of him, so I came home and said, "Cover me, cover me [with blankets]!" So they did, then Allah revealed the words:

"O you (Muhammad) enveloped in garments!
Arise and warn!
And magnify your Lord (Allah)!
And purify your garments!
And keep away from Ar-Rujz (the idols)!"
[al-Muddathir 74:1-5].'"

Abu Salamah said: *al-rujz* were the idols which the people of the Jaahiliyyah used to worship. Then the revelation came frequently after that.

(Narrated by al-Bukhaari, 4572; Muslim, 231)
al-Sira (biography of the Prophet)
****

According to the Hadith passage above, when Muhammad was overcome by these episodes, he would ask others to cover him with a blanket. Anything uttered by him would be then written down on whatever writing surface was available to them such as rocks, papyrus leaves, or even on the scapula bone of a camel. These revelations eventually formed the Quran (which literally means to recite) and often were accompanied by the ringing of a bell, sweating, shaking and sometimes foaming at the mouth almost like an epileptic seizure. In the beginning, Muhammad was very afraid, thought he was possessed by an evil spirit and tried to hurl himself off a cliff to commit suicide (Sira[3]). Once it was established by the insistence of his wife Khadija and her cousin ("the son of her paternal uncle") Waraqah that he was indeed a prophet of Allah and these were divine revelations, she became his first convert to Islam.

Waraqah (called a Christian in these Hadith accounts) is an interesting character. The passage stated that "He was a man who had become a Christian during the jaahiliyyah." The term jaahiliyyah is used to define the period of time and state of affairs in Arabia before the advent of Islam. It is usually called a "state of ignorance" and referred also to the prolific worship of idols in that area. Yet as the Hadith states, not all were polytheists- there were practicing Jews and small groups of Christians. It is generally assumed by scholars that Waraqah was most likely Nestorian in his beliefs (the Council of Ephesus rejected Nestorianism in 431 AD as heresy). There is an excellent article by the Gospel Coalition (2015) that addresses the state of affairs of Christianity before the time of Muhammad titled "The Coptic Church and Chalcedon.[4]"Even though the Hadith chronicles this exchange with Waraqah, there is no evidence that he ever converted to Islam.

---

[3] Lings, M. (2006). *Muhammad: His life based on the earliest sources*. Rochester, Vt: Inner Traditions.

[4] DeYoung, K (2015) "The Coptic Church and Chalcedon."
https://www.thegospelcoalition.org/blogs/kevin-deyoung/the-coptic-church-and-chalcedon/

Islam and Muslim can both be confusing terms. Islam is the religion founded by Muhammad. Islam is an Arabic word that means "to submit or surrender." From the Quran: "Yes [on the contrary], whoever submits his face in Islam to Allah while being a doer of good will have his reward with his Lord. And no fear will there be concerning them, nor will they grieve (Surah 2:112)."

A Muslim is one who practices or surrenders to Islam (Surah 2:136). One can become a Muslim by reciting the words of the Shahada (belief in Allah as one and Muhammad as the last prophet) in the presence of a witness or by themselves. They also follow the five pillars of faith and believe in works to earn a place in Paradise. They believe that Islam is no different than other monotheistic religions that came before except that Allah saved his final and best revelation for Muhammad through the Quran.

There are problems in the casual reading of the Quran as it is not arranged in cohesive sections like the Bible. The Quran is not even organized chronologically, but is arranged by the size of a chapter from the longest to the shortest - with the exception of Surah al Fatiha or "The Beginning." This makes it hard to follow when reading. For example, some of the revelations in Surah 2 are from Muhammad's time in Medina and some are revelations from six years later. Another source of confusion is from the practice of abrogation of replacing verses in the Quran, such as the limit of having four wives being abrogated later to make a special exemption for Muhammad to marry his adopted son's wife (Surah 33:37). Abrogation is a legal term that means to annul or abolish by authoritative action. An article by David Bukay of the Middle East Forum states:

"The Quran is unique among sacred scriptures in accepting a doctrine of abrogation in which later pronouncements of the Prophet declare null and void his earlier pronouncements. Four verses in the Quran acknowledge or justify abrogation:

- When we cancel a message, or throw it into oblivion, we replace it with one better or one similar. Do you not know that God has power over all things? [Quran 2:106]
- When we replace a message with another, and God knows best what he reveals, they say: You have made it up. Yet, most of them do not know. [Quran 16:101]
- God abrogates or confirms whatsoever he will, for he has with him the Book of the Books. [Quran 13:39]
- If we pleased, we could take away what we have revealed to you. Then you will not find anyone to plead for it with us. [Quran 17:86]

Rather than explain away inconsistencies in passages regulating the Muslim community, many jurists acknowledge the differences but accept that latter verses trump earlier verses. Most scholars divide the Quran into verses revealed by Muhammad in Mecca when his community of followers was weak and more inclined to compromise, and those revealed in Medina, where Muhammad's strength grew" (2007)[5].

The article is a great reference for anyone who might be interested in seeing how the verses in the Quran were peaceful in nature and then were subsequently changed to more violent passages that occurred during the time of the growth of Islam.

---

[5] Bukay, D (2007). "Peace or Jihad? Abrogation in Islam." *Middle East Quarterly Fall 2007 Volume 14: Number 4. Retrieved from* https://www.meforum.org/articles/2007/peace-or-jihad-abrogation-in-islam#_ftn8

The article also shows how the abrogations paralleled the power and influence of Islam in Arabia.

✝ **CONNECTION:** The Bible states several times that God does not change and is immutable. He is the same yesterday, today and forever (Hebrews 13:8).

"God is not man, that he should lie, or a son of man, that he should change his mind. Has he said, and will he not do it? Or has he spoken, and will he not fulfill it? Behold, I received a command to bless he has blessed, and I cannot revoke it. (Numbers 23:19-20) " Furthermore, the Bible also gives a warning to believers:

"Do not be deceived, my beloved brothers. Every good gift and every perfect gift is from above, coming down from the Father of lights, with whom there is no variation or shadow due to change. (James 1:16-7)"

Kaaba (the black cube)

As Islam began to gain momentum, Muhammad and his group of followers fled approximately 200 miles from Mecca to Medina in 622 AD to avoid persecution from the polytheists and to organize the first Muslim community with political and economic independence from surrounding tribes. This is called the *Hijrah,* and it marked the beginning of the Islamic Calendar. Muhammad re-established the Kaaba in Mecca 17 months after his arrival in Yathrib (Medina) as the place for Muslim pilgrimage (it used to be the location for annual pilgrimage for polytheists around Arabia). It later became the Muslim *Qibla* or direction for prayer around the world. Mecca was the seat of the mercantile Quraysh tribe - Muhammad's family came from the Banu Hashim clan.[6]

The Kaaba literally means a temple in the shape of a cube and it is the black cube one sees in the photographs of Mecca. It is considered to be the heart of Mecca as the place for the annual pilgrimage for all Muslims. Muslim scholars concur that in the time of Muhammad idolatry was rampant, with particular gods being worshiped throughout Arabia. This included Hubal (whom the Quraysh worshiped) who is often linked to Baal - one of the primary idols mentioned in the Old Testament. There were also gods called Isaf of Safa and Naila of Marwa and folklore represented them as having sexual relations in the Kaaba. The following Quran and Hadith passages record the two places as still having an important place in Islam: "Behold! Safa and Marwa **are among the symbols of Allah**. So if those who visit the House in the Season or at other times, should compass them round, it is no sin in them. And if any one obeys his own impulse to good, — be sure that Allah is He Who recognizes and knows (Surah al-Baqarah 2:158 and Hadith Sahih Bukhari 6:22-23)."

The Kaaba has its own folklore in Islam and it captures the Muslim's attention each day during prayer as its image is on most prayer rugs. I grew up with bedtime stories that recapitulated the boldness of Muhammad as he went into the Kaaba and crushed the 360 idols that were housed there.[7] In one fell swoop, he obliterated idolatry and instituted monotheism in Arabia. This was no easy task as powerful families were against him. In that day, the polytheists came in thousands to the Kaaba

---

[6] Lings, M. (2006). *Muhammad: His life based on the earliest sources*. Rochester, Vt: Inner Traditions.

[7] http://www.lastprophet.info/arabia-in-the-pre-islamic-period

to worship in an annual pilgrimage. This was a veritable source of predictable income for the Arab tribes.

Muhammad's Death and Division

Two major sects were developed right after Muhammad's death in 632 AD: the Sunni and Shi'a. **Sunnis** regard themselves as the orthodox branch of Islam. The name "**Sunni**" is derived from the phrase "Ahl al-Sunnah", or "People of the Tradition." All Muslims are guided by the Sunnah, but **Sunnis** stress its primacy. **Shia** are also guided by the wisdom of Muhammad's descendants through his son-in-law and cousin, Ali.[8]

SUNNI
- Caliphate
- Abu Bakr – Ist Caliph (do not recognize Ali as the heir)
- Follow Sunnah = Muhammad's example & are also called "People of the Tradition"
- 85-90% of the Muslim World

SHIA
- Ali = legitimate male heir
- Abu Talib (uncle) was Ali's father
- Ali married Fatimah – Muhammad's daughter
- Follow direct "descendant" of Muhammad as successor
- 6-10% of the Muslim World

✝ **CONNECTION:** Right from the start, there is confusion in the way information is presented in Islam. There is a layered approach to obtaining information from the Quran, Hadith, Sira

[8](January 2016). Sunnis and Shia: Islam's Ancient Schism. Retrieved from https://www.bbc.com/news/world-middle-east-16047709

and the resulting Shari'a laws that exist to define what a Muslim can and cannot do. Most Muslims take great pride in reading the Quran and there are celebrations held for small children who have recited the Quran from start to finish with an Imam's (a Muslim cleric) help. As a Muslim woman growing up in the United States, I did not know the existence of the Hadith. Some people own copies of the Hadith and have them in their home library. Our family owned a Quran that was not read that often but sat on a designated shelf in the main area of our house for all to see.

There are Muslims who do not know or understand all that I have presented in this first section. When connecting with a Muslim, do not assume that they are well-versed or educated in the history of Islam. It is frowned upon to use and study anything outside of the Quran for a Muslim. I was heavily discouraged from reading about Arabian history. Women are even more sheltered from information presented in the Hadith and Sira (mainly because both contain graphic language about what a man can and cannot do with women and female slaves or captives). It wasn't until after I became a Christian that I finally read the Hadith and eventually the Sira of Muhammad.

How beautiful to have God's entire revelation in the Old and New Testament of the Bible! We do not have to go to several different books or places to find out what Jesus said or meant. All we need as Christians is present in the Bible, which is "All Scripture is breathed out by God and profitable for teaching, for reproof, for correction, and for training in righteousness, that the man of God may be complete, equipped for every good work (2 Timothy 3:16)."

1. Allah is ONE - no more paganism (practice at that time in Arabia) is stated by the _____ .

2. Islam means:

   _____ .

3. Quran means: _____ .

4. Hadith are: _____ of Muhammad.

5. Sira of Muhammad is a book about the _____ of Muhammad.

6. Abrogation means _____ .

7. Sahih means _____ .

APPLICATION

What are 3 things you learned about ISLAM in this chapter?

_____

_____

_____

What does the Bible teach about the word of God in Mark 13:31?

_____

_____

How is this different than the revelations in the Quran?

_____

_____

How will you use this information to further the Gospel?

_____

_____

Chapter 2

Muslim Beliefs & Practices

Rejoice in the Lord always; again I will say, rejoice. Let your reasonableness be known to everyone. The Lord is at hand; do not be anxious about anything, but in everything by prayer and supplication with thanksgiving let your requests be made known to God. And the peace of God, which surpasses all understanding, will guard your hearts and your minds in Christ Jesus.
Philippians 4:4-7

There are FIVE Beliefs in Islam and FIVE Pillars of Faith.

Islam is systematic in nature. There are checklists and standard times to pray, verses to memorize and special methods to learn. There is a set of verses I had to memorize in Arabic (not my language) when I was young and these serve as the basis of Muslim doctrine. Several groups of verses are not found together in the Quran but some of the creed verses point to Surah al Ikhlas (Surah 112) and the Surah al Fatihah (Surah 1 - The Opener[9]). In my book "From Isa to Christ - A Muslim Woman's Search for the Hand of God," I explained in detail how

---

[9] Surah al Fatihah. https://quran.com/1

the five pillars of faith were used to help me to understand how
I had fallen short of the standards of Allah as set by Islam.

FIVE BELIEFS

The Statement of Beliefs is based on a different set of verses
in the Quran:

O you who have believed, believe in Allah and His
Messenger and the Book that He sent down upon His
Messenger and the Scripture which He sent down before.
And whoever disbelieves in Allah, His angels, His books,
His messengers, and the Last Day has certainly gone far
astray (Surah an Nisa 4:136).

The meaning of the creed is as follows:

Amantu billahi: I believe in the existence and oneness of
Allah, that He has no partners or counterparts, that He has
all kinds of loftiness and that He is free of all kinds of
deficiency.

Wa malaikatihi: I also believe in the angels of Allah.

Wa kutubihi: I also believe in the books of Allah.

Wa rusulihi: I also believe in the prophets of Allah.

Wal-yawmil-akhiri: I also believe in the Day of Judgment.

Wa bil-qadari khayrihi wa sharrihi minallahi taala: I also
believe in the destiny, that everything that seems as good

or evil to us take place through the knowledge, law and creation of Allah.

Wal-ba'thu ba'dal-mawti haqqun: I also heartily believe in life after death (and resurrection). All of them are true and right.

Ashhadu an la ilaha illallah wa ashhadu anna Muhammadan abduhu wa rasuluh: I witness that there is no god but Allah and I witness that prophet Muhammad is his slave and messenger.

The Statement of Beliefs is common knowledge for Muslims who are only culturally connected to Islam and do not practice daily prayer or other Muslim obligations. It is taught to children on their hands (one hand for the statement of beliefs and the other for the five pillars of faith). The belief in one God is also the first pillar of faith as it is the hallmark of Islamic belief. The belief in angels is not the same as in Christianity, for angels take on another supernatural meaning. They are not simply messengers of God - they will also suffer death and there are no fallen angels (such as Satan - he is a different supernatural being). Therefore, there are only good angels who do the bidding of Allah. The only archangel is Gabriel (Jibreel in Arabic) and the Quran states that he was the one who brought the revelation to Muhammad, as well as the news of the virgin birth to Mary. The Quran (Surah 32:11) mentions an angel of death, along with other angels who are responsible for recording the good and bad deeds of man on a daily basis, especially during prayer time. These are known as the "honorable scribes. There are two more named *Munkar* and *Nakeer*, who are responsible for asking people questions in the grave[10].

There are four books Muslims are told to believe in by the Quran: Taurat (or Tawrat - Torah) revealed to Musa (Moses), the Zabur (Psalms) delivered to Daud (David) and the Injil (or Injeel -New Testament Gospel) to Isa Masih or Jesus Messiah. Do Muslims ever read these other books? The answer is a firm "No!" because they believe that these books were corrupted by the Jews and Christians and therefore, Allah had to give his final revelation to Muhammad in the Quran.

The prophets Muslims believe in are many of the same ones found in the Old and New Testament, including Abraham, Joseph, Noah, Moses, Jonah, etc. There are a few extra prophets

---

[10] "Authentic Descriptions of Munkar and Nakeer" (2005).
https://islamqa.info/en/72400

the Quran adds: Adam (first human being created, but did not prophecy) and another enigmatic man named Dhul Qarnayn, which tradition says was Alexander the Great (in a commentary of the Quran, Abul Ala Maududi noted that historically most Muslim scholars did endorse the identification of Dhul-Qarnayn with Alexander the Great due to writing in Tafsir al-Jalalayn).[11]

The fifth and final belief is in Judgment Day when the good and bad deeds of Muslims will be weighed on a balance scale. Those who do not confess the Shahadah (Allah is one and Muhammad is his last prophet) will automatically go to hell (Surah Ali 'Imran 3:85). The idea of Heaven is not like the one presented in the Bible, where we are allowed to enter into the very presence of God and worship Him eternally. Heaven is a vast departure from the one in the Bible and is called "Paradise." For Muslims, it is a physical place filled with lush velvet couches, beautiful trays laden with rich food and rivers of wine. There are also women present for a man's every need (including his wives if he wants them - if not, they get only a velvet couch, food, milk, and honey). Allah is removed from it and sits above. There is no worship going on amidst the hedonism.

FIVE PILLARS

Five pillars of Islam serve as the foundational basis and a checklist for Muslims to do on a regular basis. The pillars also serve as a sign of their dedication to Islam and the Muslim's commitment to the faith. They are all based on works, except for the Shahadah (belief in one God), which is an expression of faith. These are not the five "suggestions" but are MANDATORY for all Muslims in order to get to Paradise. This

---

[11] Alexander the Great. Maududi, Abul Ala (1972). "Tafheen ul Qura'an." p.18:83, note 62.

is one area both Sunni and Shia agree upon and practice. Even cultural Muslims know that the five pillars exist as they are discussed often in mosques and are taught to little children.

First Pillar: One God - The Shahadah

The last part of the Beliefs statement makes up the first part of the five pillars. It is to say aloud in the presence of another Muslim the following words:

La ilaha illallah wa ashhadu anna Muhammadan abduhu wa rasuluh: I witness that there is no god but Allah and I witness that prophet Muhammad is his slave and messenger.

If you do this, you are automatically a Muslim. Nothing else to do, other than read the Quran, follow the rest of the pillars, and come to the mosque to meet the Muslim community (the Ummah).

Second Pillar: Prayer - Salah

Prayer as a Muslim is a difficult concept for others to understand since there are many aspects surrounding it that make it extremely formal and rigid! There are assigned times for prayer and a format to follow in Arabic ONLY -even if you don't speak Arabic as your mother tongue. The prayers are to be said at certain times of the day, with Arabic verses that go with each prayer (Rakat) and must be completed with ablutions (ritual washing to purify) before starting prayer.

There are several charts to help children learn how to pray. It is commonly taught that if a child does not pray and fast by the age of ten, the parents should beat them. Prayer is not a time to get closer to Allah. It is obligatory and serves to set a pattern for the Muslim's day.

When I first learned how to pray, it was like taking an entire course. I was given a table of prayers that showed me when to pray and how many prayers to recite. At first glance, the table of requirements for prayer looks like it belonged in a math book. I have included it here to visually show how many requirements there are for the Muslim who tries to pray daily. From the table, there are a few words that need to be defined: Rakat: a set of verses from the Quran that are prayed in Arabic, Sunnat: what Muhammad performed, Farz (or Fard): mandatory, Nafl: voluntary (do as many as you like), Witr: what Muhammad encouraged all Muslims to perform. Between what is mandatory to what is recommended or even urged by Muhammad, there are a large number of verse sets (Rakat) to be performed! The Muslim who does not speak Arabic must learn an entire new set of vocabulary just to do their prayers and fulfill this pillar. It is a big undertaking, considering prayer is first taught to a child around the age of seven.

The Rakats on the table show that the morning prayer time is the shortest in length, while the evening prayer can be four times the amount of verses. This allowance was given by Muhammad for people who had to work, assuming that there was more time allotted in the evening for prayer.

Arabic	English Meaning	Explanation
Rakat	Set of Verses	From Quran to be said in Arabic
Sunnat	Muhammad's example	Hadith & pattern for prayer set by the prophet of Islam
Farz/Fard	Mandatory	If you skip these sets of prayers, it is a sin
Nafl	Voluntary	Do as many as you like for extra credit
Witr	Cord of a Circle - believed to close out the day and bring you into the next day	Encouraged prayer by Muhammad- to be performed after the evening prayer and before the sunrise prayer (for great merit)

	Table of Prayer Rakats						
	Sunnat	Farz	Sunnat	Nafl	Witr	Nafl	Total Rakat
Prayer Time							
Fajr before sunrise	2	2					**4**
Zohr after 12:00 pm	4	4	2	2			**12**
Asr afternoon	4	4					**8**
Maghrib after sunset		3	2	2			**7**
Isha dusk to dawn	4	4	2	2	3	2	**17**
Jumuah Friday	4	2	4+2	2			**14**

Rakat Table made by Mona Sabah ©(2018)

This was certainly the case for me when I was trying to be a devout Muslim. When I was able to wake up in time for the morning prayers (the required set of ablutions and all Rakats were to be performed before sunrise), it would take me about thirty to forty five minutes to complete. The evening time was a different matter as it took me almost two and a half hours to get through my prayers. This was my struggle daily, along with trying to get children ready for school and myself ready for work. Now, granted, it does not take most Muslims that long to pray daily. I know people who race through it all, completing the requirements in a quarter of the time it used to take me.

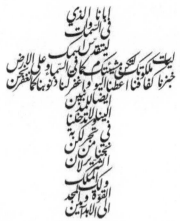

The Lord's prayer in Arabic

Christian Prayer

*Pray in the Spirit at all times , with every prayer & petition
(Ephesians 6:18)*
Pray without ceasing (1 Thessalonians 5:17)
*Rejoice in hope, be patient in tribulation, be constant in prayer
(Romans 12:12)*
*And when you pray, do not babble on like pagans, for they think
that by their many words they will be heard (Mathew 6:7)*

✝ **CONNECTION:** We have an amazing freedom in Christ that we take for granted at times. We can pray anywhere we want, in any direction, and any way we want. I was very confused as a new Christian when people would sing at church. I did not understand that singing was a form of worship to the Lord. I did not realize that singing hymns and songs of praise in the car was allowed. It is a beautiful way to introduce to your Muslim friend how the LORD gives His adopted children to access Him at all times. We are welcomed freely to the throne of God through the blood and covering of our Lord Jesus. Even when we don't have the words to say or are weak, the Holy Spirit will intercede for us (Romans 8:26). In this way, we get to experience the Trinity of God... praying to God, through intercession of Christ with the power of the Holy Spirit. No wonder prayer for the believer is POWER!

Third Pillar: Fasting - Sawm for Ramadan

Fasting (Sawm) during Ramadan is the third pillar of Islam. Sawm doesn't have to be done at Ramadan and a Muslim can fast at any time. Fasting during Ramadan, however, is mandatory and expected according to Islamic law. Surah Al Baqara 2:183 says "Believers! Fasting is enjoined upon you, as it was enjoined upon those before you, that you become God-fearing." At first, Muhammad called all Muslims to fast at least three days a month outside of Ramadan. Later, the rule was relaxed and no longer became an obligation for his followers. If a Muslim missed a day, they could give charity to a poor person to make up the missed day of fasting. The rules are also relaxed to accommodate the sick, pregnant, nursing mothers and elderly.

Imams teach that fasting is for a fixed number of days, and if one of you is sick, or if one of you are on a journey, you will fast the same number of other days later on. For those who are capable of fasting (but still do not fast) there is a redemption: "feeding a needy man for each day missed. Whoever voluntarily does more good than is required, will find it better for him; and that you should fast is better for you, if you only know (Surah Al Baqara 2:184).[12]"All (except for those who have not yet reached puberty, any who are traveling, the elderly and infirm) are supposed to fast, as Ramadan is a holy month for Muslims. If women are menstruating, nursing or bleeding from childbirth, they are excused from fasting during that time, but are expected to make up their fasts so they do not sin. In this way, women are always falling in spiritual debt, falling behind in their requirements to be a Muslim.

Fasting for Muslims is to abstain from all things impure: lying, cheating, sexual desires, eating and drinking during the daylight hours. That means many Muslims can feast during the night - so you are actually exchanging daytime eating for night. In different countries and cultures, there are differing views on the reason for Ramadan. Some wonder if it is to try to draw closer to Allah and gain his pleasure? Since Allah is seen as a Master and humans as the slave, there is a deep desire to please Allah only. This is also another reason for fasting. The more humanitarian view is that it allows Muslims to have compassion on the poor and needy by feeling the hunger they feel during the day. An Egyptian Muslim said it is for the poor to be remembered, while an Algerian said it was not about hunger at all but more about obedience to Allah.

In some Islamic countries during Ramadan, the price of food increases markedly (maybe to have people avoid purchasing food during the day?). This would make it even harder for the poor and needy to eat. I was told a story by a friend about a Muslim woman she knew who came to the United

[12] Surah al Baqara
http://www.islamicstudies.info/tafheem.php?sura=2&verse=183&to=184

States. During Thanksgiving, her Muslim friend feared that the price of food would increase like it did in her country for Ramadan, but was surprised to see the opposite happened!

My own experience was different because when I was growing up in Muslim countries, there was a party atmosphere at night. The whole neighborhood would stay awake and we would try to gorge ourselves until the last possible moment right before sunrise. In the evenings, it was a wonderful time of gathering, community and of course, eating. As a Muslim, I was told that Ramadan was strictly for Allah to test your obedience to him. It was to test your endurance and to see how strong you were. I failed miserably! As an adult, I would get ferocious migraines and to my shame, I had to go and get a doctor's note so I would have an excuse not to fast when asked by friends or family. Not fasting is not an option for a Muslim. The only valid excuses are if a woman is menstruating (but then they have to make up the missed days) or if you have a medical reason.

Over the last few years, there has been an increase of newspaper articles focused on the charity of Muslim volunteers at local food banks during the month of Ramadan. What most don't understand is that this is not done out of the overflow of a grateful heart for the grace of God - instead, Ramadan is a focused time where Muslims accumulate their good deed credits.

It is a tough system for a Muslim to follow - they never know how much is in their spiritual bank account. There is no calculator for how much a good deed is worth verses another and the same holds true for bad deeds - no Muslim knows how much each sin costs as a debit recorded on the final scales of Judgment Day.

✝ **CONNECTION:** Christians also fast and pray. Jesus addressed fasting in the New Testament - not as an obligation but as a way to bring us closer to the heart of God. When we fast, we are not to announce it to the world, but to do this between us and God. Also, since days and nights are flipped for Muslim fasting, it is not evident to them that everyone fasts daily (we don't eat at night but do in the waking hours - that's why it's called "breakfast!"). In contrast, the Christian fast does not make up any meals or transpose the day for night. It is more of a solitary endeavor to help us seek the wisdom of God. There are several Christian websites that engage in 30 days of deep prayer for the Muslim world during Ramadan. I have done this many times and find that it is encouraging and uplifting to have my Christian brothers and sisters praying for salvation for the Muslims through Jesus.

Another thing to note is that some Muslims use fasting as a shield of protection from the evil spirits. We can again introduce them to Jesus Christ's teaching in Matthew "But this kind never comes out except by prayer and fasting" (Matthew 17:21). It is the power of Christ through the Holy Spirit that helps us to overcome evil. Fasting is a trying time for Muslims especially in Western countries where donuts are available for morning meetings, business lunches or others eating at school in the cafeteria, etc. It is a kind act to look out for your Muslim friend during this time and to give them some grace by not discussing your delicious lunch plans or even refraining from eating in front of them. I do not encourage Christians to fast during Ramadan as a show of solidarity because Muslims fast in order to gain good deeds and earn their favor with Allah for admission to Paradise. We do not believe in works for salvation. We believe in the only atoning work of Jesus Christ.

Another place for a connection is at the evening meal after a day of fasting. Several of my Christian friends have been invited to come and break the fast (called Iftar or Iftari) in the evening. They usually are not sure what to do. My view always keeps the Gospel in the forefront. Does it open the door to share the Gospel with others? There is a fine line between attending, participating and joining a Muslim in prayer. I would most definitely draw the line at joining in prayer. During the Muslim prayer time, you may excuse yourself, go outside and pray in the name of Jesus for the whole house, you can do that OR you can stand in the back and pray for the Lord to move amongst the people.

The Iftar meal is usually just a party intended to get the community together -- that has been the case in all the ones I have attended in different countries over the course of my life. Offer to help with the food preparation and serve your Muslim friend. There may be a short prayer recited over the food, but not many lengthy prayers, as most are absolutely starving! The short prayer will be followed by breaking of the fast with dates and water (tradition). Then the feasting begins. Another piece of advice is for the Christian women to dress modestly (cover arms & legs - jeans are alright), and bring a scarf or a shawl in case they would like you to cover your head. There is nothing Biblically wrong with covering or uncovering your hair. I personally think it is a sign of respect and consideration for the custom if you come prepared with a head covering. Another polite suggestion is to bring a gift for the person hosting, especially if this is your first visit to their home. Usually, I recommend something sweet like a cake, cookies or something to share with others. This way, you detour all the halal regulations as well as bring food to show your host your gratitude for the invitation.

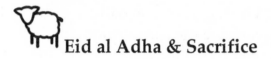

Eid al Adha & Sacrifice

At the conclusion of the annual fasting days of Ramadan, there is a small celebration called Eid al Fitr (same Arabic root word for breaking a fast - iftar) and then a large celebration 70 days later that calls for a sacrifice. It is called Eid al Aha or the Festival of the Sacrifice. One day, a man visited our home in Pakistan and he brought along the sweetest thing I had ever seen in my life. We were not allowed to have our own pets. We had a guard dog, but the guard (sometimes chauffeur) used to feed, pet, and keep the dog. We played with him sometimes, but it was greatly frowned upon by my nanny who insisted on scrubbing us down if we even touched the dog, since dogs are considered dirty in Islam.

The man brought something even more special than a dog... he had a rope in his hand and at the end of that rope was a fluffy little lamb. It had a sweet face and just stared at us, chewing on whatever it was in his mouth. My parents took the lamb from him and thanked him. My older sister immediately fell in love with it and said that she would only feed it flowers, for it was too precious to eat just plain straw and grass that the man had brought along with him. She took the lamb's leash and ran off to the heavily flowered garden in front of our home where she stayed true to her promise for the next few weeks.

Each day, we played with the lamb until we got used to its presence. It would roam around our home and three gardens (one at the front, one in the middle between our house and annex and another one at the back of the annex). I remember just sitting outside, watching it roam around and eat a few nibbles from my hand. Never did we question where this gift came from or why my parents had suddenly decided to get us a lamb as a pet. We simply enjoyed it.

Early one morning, I awoke to a very loud noise of someone crying... no, it was almost like a child's scream. I jumped out of bed, scared to death. The screaming and crying noise would not go away. I ran out of the house, still in my pajamas, and followed the horrific sounds as they were coming from the back garden. As I approached, I knew something was terribly wrong. There were men with beards standing around the back faucet, where we had a small concrete basin for washing off yard dirt or larger, messy chores.

One of the men saw me staring with eyes as large as saucers at the scene. He hollered at our cook "Get her out of here!" as I started to scream and cry in horror. For I saw what had been making the noise. It was our beloved lamb. There was blood pouring out everywhere – the wash basin, the ground and on the two men who had done the sacrifice. In the middle was our lamb with its neck sliced wide open. Blood drenched its body as well. I realized then that it was a lamb my parents had bought for Eid Al-Adha which all Muslims celebrate with a sacrifice of a lamb 70 days after the end of Ramadan and after sighting of a new moon according to a Lunar Calendar. Never had I given it any thought of the lamb that was to be sacrificed for our party meal.

This is something still practiced all around the world by Muslims. Eid Al-Adha is the festival to remember Abraham's obedience to God to sacrifice his son (we won't argue which son it is right now…). It is a celebration that allows families to come together and give thanks to Allah. My parents still pay for a lamb to be sacrificed in Pakistan and the meat to be distributed to charity.

In the book of Revelation 5:6, there is a passage that says that *"And between the throne and the four living creatures and among the elders I saw a Lamb standing, as though it had been slain, with seven horns and with seven eyes, which are the seven spirits of God sent out into all the earth."* As I read this verse, I realized that the Lord showed me already what it must have looked like to have a lamb slain - I thought back to the bloody scene I witnessed as a child.

One of the things I have noticed most about living in the United States is that everything is neat and tidy. While we lived in a nice home in Pakistan, we weren't always guaranteed clean water out of the faucet. I remember being quite upset several times when I turned on the faucet for my bath and the water ran brown. We don't like to think of the blood or the guts. We like things to be sanitary. We get our meat nicely packaged at the grocery store. Our streets are clean, our water comes out of the faucet clear, our clothes are clean and we have hand sanitizers in every location. It's not considered polite to discuss the gory details of any event, especially dealing with blood - even sometimes the blood of Christ spilled for us on the cross.

✝ **CONNECTION:** What a beautiful place to connect to the GOSPEL!

Our treatment of Jesus' sacrifice should not be sanitized. We need to accept the fact that it was a bloody mess and a thing of horror. We should accept the fact that He suffered and he felt every bit of the pain on the Cross. As we annually look at Good Friday as the day that commemorates Jesus on the Cross, we need to remember that He was the lamb that was slain from the foundation of the world (Rev. 13:8 and 1 Peter 1:20). Our Lord gave up every drop of blood for us. The least we can do is to acknowledge His sacrifice for us in the way it happened... not as a sanitized version of the cross, but a cross full of God's glory and His willingness to provide for us a spotless, sinless lamb who takes away the sins of the world. Amen.

Christ = True Obedience & True Sacrifice
Sinless Lamb of God (John 1:29)
True Sacrifice
Worthy is the Lamb (Revelation 5:12)
Lamb Slain from the Foundation of the World
(Revelation 13:8)

Fourth Pillar: Giving Alms - Zakat

Zakat[13] in Arabic means purification and also growth for a Muslim. In the Quran, Zakat is called "Sadaqat" to mean charity or alms. The Surah Tauba 9:103 states "(O Mohammed) take out of their possessions Sadaqat so that you may cleanse and purify them thereby, and pray for them..."

Many Muslims (including my parents and their Sunni tradition) choose to give 2.5% of their income for Zakat, but this is not stated very clearly (some say it is not stated at all) in the Quran[14]. A rule of thumb is that a person should give whatever they feel like giving. If an occasion called for a large gift of charity, they could do that or even give a small amount for a friend. It is up to the Muslim on what they wish to give. According to the National Foundation[15] for Zakat, charity is sometimes (not always) given out of guilt as an offering to make up for lack of fasting, lying or cheating. So, it's not always clear why charity is being given - other than as a requirement and a credit for the good and bad deeds account.

Fifth Pillar: The Pilgrimage - Hajj

Hajj is the fifth pillar and is a sacred requirement for all Muslims. It is performed in the last month of the Muslim calendar and pilgrims from all over the world, including

---

[13] "Zakat." http://www.islam-guide.com/ch3-16.htm#footnote1
[14] see http://islamqa.info/en/145600
[15] "Objective of Zakat." http://www.nzf.org.uk/Knowledge/ObjectiveOfZakat

people of all social standings attend (Quran -Al Hajj Surah 22 verse 27). It is not uncommon to see poor people walking alongside royalty. Hajj takes about five days to perform. It is an enormous undertaking for the person and for the nation of Saudi Arabia, as over two million people come annually to fulfill the obligation of this pillar.

There are several rituals that are an important part of Hajj, namely clothing, prayers, special restrictions, manner in which to perform it and includes a special way to indicate when a pilgrim has fulfilled these requirements. Chapter 22 in the Quran, titled Surah Al Hajj, states that all who are able should undertake the pilgrimage to the Kaaba in Mecca. You only have to perform this once in your lifetime, but there are many who make the pilgrimage more than once.

The Hadith promises great rewards for those who perform Hajj - "when you return from the pilgrimage, all your sins are washed clean[16] -- for a little while. There are also different types of Hajj that can be performed with a litany of details and differences in the rites associated with each. There is Hajj-e-Tamattu, Hajj-e-Qiran and a special Hajj designated only for the residents of Mecca called Hajj-e-Ifrad.

There are special clothes one is required to wear when performing the Hajj pilgrimage. This is called "Ihram" in Arabic and it means "consecration" or to do something holy. It is a requirement as stated in the Hadith because the checklist for performing Hajj is not found in the Quran. When we lived in Saudi Arabia and went to perform the pilgrimage as a family, my parents packed food, water,

---

[16] Hadith 1521, Book of Hajj, Bukhari, Vol. 2

sandals for our feet and other safety items. All travelers are required by the government to limit the amount of money or valuables they bring. No jewelry, watches or accessories are allowed on women or men. The moment a Muslim puts on the Ihram (white clothes), they are finally given the honorific title of "Muhrim" or "Haji" for one who performs the Hajj.

At the Kaaba Muslims begin what's called "Tawaf." It means to walk and circle the Kaaba counter clockwise seven times. You will see the term "circumambulation" noted for this activity - it simply means to walk around in a circle in a ceremonious manner. The Imams teach that the pattern of walking around the Kaaba mimics the planetary movements.

In the eastern-most corner of the Kaaba is a black stone, set in silver called the Hajar al aswad. Islamic tradition holds that it was a meteorite that had fallen from the sky and that Muhammad himself set it into the Kaaba. As mentioned in chapter one, the Kaaba originally housed hundreds of pagan idols and their sacred black stone appeared years before Muhammad claimed the Kaaba for worship of only Allah[17]. The black cloth covering has inscriptions of the Quran embroidered with gold thread and is changed every two years. The Kaaba remains the iconic symbol of Islam and is recognized around the world.

To start the Tawaf , the pilgrim should start at a brown marble line on the floor and try to touch or kiss the black stone. There is a great deal of jostling that takes place at this point. As a small child, my dad put me upon his shoulders and allowed me to touch, feel and kiss the smooth black

---

stone as he did. He also explained to me there that it was a touch that went back centuries and connected Muslims to the prophet Muhammad and even earlier to the prophet Abraham (some call the stone encasement "Abraham's station"). The Hajj includes other rituals and stops at designated places around the Kaaba in order to recite prayer verses for each round.

 Jihad

Sometimes called the "6th Pillar," jihad is an Arabic word that denotes a religious duty imposed on Muslims to spread Islam by waging war. It has come to denote any conflict waged for principle or belief and is often translated to mean "holy war." The literal meaning in Arabic is to struggle or to strive with an effort. This means that a Muslim can struggle with infidels as Muhammad did much of his life in Arabia through waging war on other tribes, clans and people or it can mean an internal struggle. In his article "What does Jihad mean?" author Douglas Streusand explains this concept further:

"In *hadith* collections, jihad means armed action; for example, the 199 references to jihad in the most standard collection of *hadith, Sahih al-Bukhari,* all assume that jihad means warfare.[7] More broadly, Bernard Lewis [*The Political Language of Islam* (Chicago: University of Chicago Press, 1988)] finds that "the overwhelming majority of classical theologians, jurists, and traditionalists [i.e., specialists in the *hadith*] . . . understood the obligation of jihad in a military sense."

These figures formed one distinct interpretation of jihad as war and Ibn Taymiya and his followers formed another. For the jurists, jihad fits a context of the world divided into Muslim and non-Muslim zones, *Dar al-Islam* (Abode of Islam) and *Dar al-Harb* (Abode of War) respectively. This model implies perpetual warfare between Muslims and non-Muslims until the territory under Muslim control absorbs what is not, an attitude that perhaps reflects the optimism that resulted from the quick and far-reaching Arab conquests. Extending Dar al-Islam does not mean the annihilation of all non-Muslims, however, nor even their necessary conversion. Indeed, jihad cannot imply conversion by force, for the Qur'an (2:256) specifically states "there is no compulsion in religion." Jihad has an explicitly political aim: the establishment of Muslim rule, which in turn has two benefits: it articulates Islam's supersession of other faiths and creates the opportunity for Muslims to create a just political and social order."[18]

In my own experience, I have had Muslims throw down the Crusades as a trump card as a way to say that Christians have had their own religious wars. This claim may leave some Christians at a loss on how to counter the fact of the Crusades. However, it is important to note that the Crusades ended a long time ago, while Jihad has continued since the time of Muhammad that included his army's focused attacks on the Christian Byzantine empire (at the Battle of Mu'tah). Islam has roots of warfare where the followers of Muhammad made no distinction between religion and government. According to tradition, in 629 Muhammad sent

---

[18] Streusand, D (1997). "What does jihad mean?" *Middle East Quarterly Volume 4: Number 3*. Retrieved from https://www.meforum.org/articles/other/what-does-jihad-mean

off 3,000 men to fight 100,000 Byzantines in what is modern day Jordan to ward off the unbelieving Christians who did not subscribe to his claims as a prophet. The Battle of Mu'tah ended when both sides retreated.

"Narrated 'Aisha and 'Abdullah bin 'Abbas: When the last moment of the life of Allah's Apostle came he started putting his 'Khamisa' on his face and when he felt hot and short of breath he took it off his face and said, "May Allah curse the Jews and Christians for they built the places of worship at the graves of their Prophets." The Prophet was warning (Muslims) of what those had done" from Sahih al-Bukhari *1:8:427, 1:12:749 , 4:55:657-8 7:63:209, 7:72:836.*

There are several lists of killings ordered by Muhammad during his military career that are readily available. The voluminous Hadith (also available online) account several killings and murders ordered by Muhammad, including poets named Asma bint Marwan and Abu Afak, among others who criticized and made fun of him (Sira). Some say that these instances were done in self-defense but the evidence points towards the violent inclination of Jihad.

Islam (Dar al Islam - house of submission) considers all those who are not Muslims to be a part of the Dar al Harb (abode or house of war). This is a part of what Muhammad was fighting for in his battles - to create one Islamic state, complete with caliphs who rule with power through Islamic Sharia laws. Cultural and well-meaning Muslims may not know the history behind the concept of Jihad, so we may want to consider this in our conversations.

Jihad is a "hot button" topic for both Muslims and Christians - Muslims get uncomfortable when trying to explain it to others (or will flat out deny what it means) and Christians can get fixated on the implications of it. As Christians, we need to understand that *Jihad is the only guaranteed way for Muslims to get to Paradise.* It is like the fast, express lane which allows them to bypass all the other commands and laws to keep. If a Muslim dies while fighting for Allah, he goes straight to Paradise:"So let those fight in the cause of Allah who sell the life of this world for the Hereafter. And he who fights in the cause of Allah and is killed or achieves victory - We will bestow upon him a great reward. (Surah an Nisa 4:74)." When one is a devout Muslim who is trying to do their best to please God and being oppressed by the sheer weight of all the laws that need to be fulfilled perfectly, it can be daunting. I did not feel the heavy yoke around my neck until after September 11, 2001 when I decided to practice Islam and learn more about it. That's when the laws, checklists and the burden to work up to heaven became real.

"O you who have believed, shall I guide you to a transaction that will save you from a painful punishment? [It is that] you believe in Allah and His Messenger and strive (Jihad) in the cause of Allah with your wealth and your lives. That is best for you, if you should know.

He will forgive for you your sins and admit you to gardens beneath which rivers flow and pleasant dwellings in gardens of perpetual residence. That is the great attainment. (Surah al Maidah 61:10-12)."

Martyrs exist in both Islam and Christianity. There is a fundamental difference between the two because for centuries, Christian martyrs have given up their lives under severe persecution - not in the process of declaring war today or killing others along with them but due to their testimony about Christ's resurrection.

Of key importance is that Jesus never taught violence or war, whereas the Quran commands violence against enemies in several passages (9:5, 30 38–39, 41). The Quran is absolutely **prescriptive** because it tells its believers what they should be doing yesterday, today and tomorrow. It is supposed to be applied to present day, just as it was during the time of Muhammad. In stark contrast, Jesus reprimanded His own disciple Peter in the Garden of Gethsemane when he cut off the ear of the soldier Malchus during the arrest of Christ. " *Then Simon Peter, having a sword, drew it and struck the high priest's servant and cut off his right ear. (The servant's name was Malchus.) So Jesus said to Peter, "Put your sword into its sheath; shall I not drink the cup that the Father has given me? (John 18:10)."*

The Bible is **descriptive**. While we have Old Testament passages that describe killing, it is in relation to understanding the Lord's attributes of holiness, righteousness, long-suffering and justice. The prescribed conquests of Canaan were limited and regional (unlike jihad), and foretold by prophecy. It was God's righteous judgment against a particular nation's idolatry and wickedness, but even then he was merciful. He intended his people to be a witness, a "light to the nations" of the one true God, welcoming the Rahabs (fallen women) and the Ruths (righteous women), and ultimately bringing salvation through Jesus Christ to all both Jew and Gentile who believe. This divine patience can be seen in the New Testament, as Jesus taught all His followers to pray for those who persecute them.

"You have heard that it was said, 'you shall love your neighbor and hate your enemy.' "But I say to you, love your enemies and

pray for those who persecute you, so that you may be sons of your Father who is in heaven; for He causes His sun to rise on the evil and the good and sends rain on the righteous and the unrighteous. "For if you love those who love you, what reward do you have? Do not even the tax collectors do the same? "If you greet only your brothers, what more are you doing than others? Do not even the Gentiles do the same? "Therefore you are to be perfect, as your heavenly Father is perfect." (Matthew 5:43-48).

Muslims will also bring up the Old Testament passages like Psalm 137 – where Israel weeps (as Babylonian captives) and asks the Lord to be freed through utter destruction of Babylon, including killing of babies. Again, the call went out to the LORD for one purpose - not to destroy everyone who stood in their way from that time until the present, but to free them from a certain group of oppressors. A passage that has come up in discussion with other non-believers is Matthew 10:34 -"Do not think that I have come to bring peace to the earth. I have not come to bring peace, but a sword." The sword of God is mentioned very clearly in Ephesians 6:10-20 - the Whole Armor of God:

"Finally, be strong in the Lord and in the strength of his might. Put on the whole armor of God, that you may be able to stand against the schemes of the devil. For we do not wrestle against flesh and blood, but against the rulers, against the authorities, against the cosmic powers over this present darkness, against the spiritual forces of evil in the heavenly places. Therefore take up the whole armor of God, that you may be able to withstand in the evil day, and having done all, to stand firm. Stand therefore, having fastened on the belt of truth, and having put on the breastplate of righteousness, and, as shoes for your feet, having put on the readiness given by the gospel of peace. In all circumstances take

up the shield of faith, with which you can extinguish all the flaming darts of the evil one; and take the helmet of salvation, and the sword of the Spirit, which is the word of God, praying at all times in the Spirit, with all prayer and supplication. To that end, keep alert with all perseverance, making supplication for all the saints, and also for me, that words may be given to me in opening my mouth boldly to proclaim the mystery of the gospel, for which I am an ambassador in chains, that I may declare it boldly, as I ought to speak."

✝ **CONNECTION:** The Armor of God is not physical armor with which we fight, but we fight the spiritual battle. We do not fight for victory as Christians - we fight *from a position of victory* that has already been accomplished by Christ! This is something Muslims don't know about or understand. Our fight is not against flesh and blood, but against darkness. Let's not get into fruitless arguments about war, terrorist attacks or things of this world but to help others see the love we have for the lost. As a Muslim, I was taught that when I went to sleep, I died for a little while. It was Allah's good will and pleasure to wake me up again in the morning. The Quran states "Allah takes the souls at the time of their death, and those that do not die [He takes] during their sleep. Then He keeps those for which He has decreed death and releases the others for a specified term. Indeed in that are signs for a people who give thought. (Surah 39:42)." The thought that Allah took my soul every night caused me to stay up all hours of the night with anxiety and fear on many occasions when I had been convicted of my sin. For the Muslim, there is no guarantee or assurance of salvation, except Jihad. That is a terrible way to live... and die.

1. Muslims have to pray five times a day and these prayers can be anything they want to say to Allah.   TRUE OR FALSE

2. Fasting during Ramadan means no food or water between _____ and _____.

3. _____ is the name of the Festival of Sacrifice done _____ days after the end of Ramadan.

4. The Hajj is the fifth pillar of faith and all Muslims must go to _____ at least once in their lifetime.

5. Muslims pray in _____ (language).

6. Muslims have to do all five pillars as a requirement of their religion   TRUE OR FALSE

7. Jihad is one of the 5 Pillars of Islam.   TRUE OR FALSE

8. Jihad means to _____ or _____.

APPLICATION

What are the 5 Pillars of Faith in Islam?

_____

_____

_____

_____

_____

Why are the 5 Pillars and 5 Beliefs important in our understanding of Islam?

_____

_____

How does Muslim Prayer differ from Christian Prayer?

_____

_____

How would you connect Eid al Adha to Christ's SACRIFICE for a Muslim?

_____

_____

Chapter 3

Traditions & Convictions

But thanks be to God, who in Christ always leads us in triumphal procession, and through us spreads the fragrance of the knowledge of him everywhere.

2 Corinthians 2:14

Those who are not of the Muslim faith often find their traditions and convictions confusing. It is difficult even for a Muslim to distinguish between teachings of the Quran and tradition or to figure out what is simply an attribute or folklore from the particular culture. Many foreigners who visit Muslim countries blunder over customs they did not know about. This section is intended as a resource for those who intend to go overseas or anyone wishing to invite Muslims into their homes.

Start with the name of Allah before eating

Many Muslims start with a statement of Quranic expression "Bismillah al-Rahman al-Rahim" which is Arabic for, "I start with the name of Allah who is most gracious and merciful." This is a custom for starting anything: taking an examination, starting a car, beginning your day, and of course, at the start of the meal. Sometimes, the statement is said out loud and other times, it is said quietly to themselves.

✝ **CONNECTION:** Christians also say a prayer at a meal or at the start of a journey. This is a good time to ask your Muslim friend if you can pray for their needs. Many will be surprised that you also follow a similar custom and may appreciate the offer of prayer.

Right Hand & Foot

The use of the *right* hand and foot are traditions set by Muhammad. The left is considered unclean and belonging to Satan. The left hand is also used for bathroom duties, so it is the right hand that is extended in greeting and used for eating. There is sometimes great consternation in Muslim families when children are born left-handed or seem to favor the left hand. This was the case in my own family when my children favored their left hand and their grandparents openly frowned upon the use of the left hand for eating.

Newborn Traditions

This tradition comes from a Hadith (Abu Raafi's hadith in Sunan at-Tirmidhi) that Muhammad recited a prayer in the ear of his daughter Fatima's newborn son Hussain. The prayer in the ear is the same call to prayer that one can hear from the minarets (towers) of a mosque.- called adhan or azan. Muslims believe in circumcision also, but not as an Abrahamic covenantal practice (they would not know what that was). They do it because it is considered to be a tradition that Abraham followed for cleanliness. The Hadith passage below refers to a "ransom" but there is nothing further in the Quran or the Hadith that explains what might require a ransom.

The Hadith also recounts a tradition called Tahneek (putting something sweet in a baby's mouth so they will have a sweet life) as well as performing Aqeeqah (circumcision of a newborn boy).

****

There follows an outline of what should be done on the day of the child's birth, and after that:

It is mustahabb to do tahneek for the baby and to pray for him. It was reported that Abu Moosa said: "I had a baby boy, and I brought him to the Prophet (peace and blessings of Allaah be upon him). He named him Ibraaheem, did Tahneek with some dates and prayed for Allaah to bless him, then he gave him back to me" (Narrated by al-Bukhari, 5150; Muslim, 2145). Tahneek means putting something sweet, such as dates or honey, in the child's mouth when he is first born. It is permissible to name the child on the first day or on the seventh.

It was reported that Anas ibn Maalik said: the Messenger of Allaah (peace and blessings of Allaah be upon him) said: "A boy was born to me this night and I have named him with the name of my father Ibraaheem" (Narrated by Muslim, 3126).

It was reported that 'Aa'ishah said: the Messenger of Allaah (peace and blessings of Allaah be upon him) did 'aqeeqah for al-Hasan and al-Husayn on the seventh day, and gave them their names. (Narrated by Ibn Hibbaan, 12/127; al-

Haakim, 4/264. Classed as saheeh by al-Haafiz Ibn Hajar in Fath al-Baari, 9/589).

Aqeeqah and circumcision

It was reported from Salmaan ibn 'Aamir (may Allah be pleased with him) that the Prophet (peace and blessings of Allah be upon him) said: "For the boy there should be an 'aqeeqah. Slaughter (an animal) for him and remove the harmful thing [i.e., the foreskin] from him." (Narrated by al-Tirmidhi, 1515; al-Nasaa'i, 4214; Abu Dawood, 2839; Ibn Maajah, 3164. The hadeeth was classed as saheeh by al-Albaani, may Allaah have mercy on him, in *al-Irwaa'*, 4/396).

It was reported that Samurah ibn Jundub (may Allah be pleased with him) said: the Messenger of Allah (peace and blessings of Allah be upon him) said: "A boy is ransomed by his 'aqeeqah. Sacrifice should be made for him on the seventh day, he should be given a name and his head should be shaved." (Narrated by al-Tirmidhi, 1522; al-Nasaa'i, 4220 and Abu Dawood, 2838.[19]

****

Most Muslims do not have a choice in accepting Islam. If they are born into a Muslim family, they are automatically a Muslim - especially when there is a prayer said in the baby's ear. Several Hadith report that Muhammad said *all* children were born Muslim and that it was their parents' choice to make them Jewish or the follower of another religion. When my older sons were born, my father performed this prayer in each of our boys' ears. If a child's father was a Muslim, then

---

[19] Islamic actions for welcoming a new baby (2007) https://islamqa.info/en/7889.

they are deemed to be a Muslim (it is widely accepted that a wife's religion is automatically the husband's religion). If they are born in a Muslim country, their birthplace automatically makes them a Muslim.

A Watering Can in Bathroom

There's a story I like to share with others that highlights differences in Eastern and Western culture. When I met my future husband, I was not allowed to date as a Muslim woman, so I kept our relationship a secret from my parents. It was not until after we were married that my husband finally had the chance to get to know my family and the customs we took for granted.

During one of the initial visits to their home, he came out of the bathroom with a confused look. Shaking his head, he asked me "How come there's a watering can in the bathroom and no plants around? In fact, I went and found that every single bathroom has a watering can behind the toilet. Why are there so many watering cans while the only live plants I see are outside?"

Westerners do not know that there are watering cans placed in bathrooms of many Muslim and Southeast Asian homes for what I call "bathroom duties." In these countries, there is no toilet paper. Toilet paper is an absolute luxury, especially in places where one cannot even find a small trickle of running water. In Sharia law, there is allowance made to wipe with stones after relieving oneself. In Pakistan, the watering can is called a "lota." There was a news article several years ago about some Muslims who were detained at an Orlando airport because they were lingering in the bathroom and had asked someone for a cup to do ritual washings.[20] The poor man explained to authorities that he needed the cup for "istinja" which is the Arabic word for washing the private parts after using the bathroom.

No bottom of feet

Feet are considered unclean in many eastern countries and religions (such as Judaism). The same holds true for Islam. Resting with the bottom of your feet facing another person is a downright insult and shows disrespect to another. This is why many Muslims will be found sitting on their feet on the floor or sitting with the legs crossed. It is also believed that one should never sleep with the bottom of the feet pointed towards Mecca. All beds should point away, as this is a sign of respect for the Qibla (direction of prayer - towards the Kaaba).

Taking off one's shoes in the home is also another consideration in many Asian cultures, although in the United States not many expect Western visitors to abide by this tradition. At the mosque, no shoes are worn for prayer and care is taken to keep the feet clean and pointed away from people and prayer areas. There is great vigilance in protecting the ablutions done before prayer time so they do not become null and void. When visiting a Muslim home, you should take your cue at the front door. If you see a bunch of shoes sitting around, then ask the host if you should remove your shoes. If you do not, it may be safe to assume this is not required of you. When in doubt, just ask!

---

[20] Hughes, Tammy (2012). "Group of Muslims Detained at Orlando Airport after asking for a cup on board a plane." www.dailymail.co.uk/news/article-2152332/Group-Muslims-detained-police-Orlando-airport-asking-cup-board-plane.html

No alcohol or pork

Alcohol is expressly forbidden in Islam. There is no exception... that is until you get to Paradise. Then you can have all the alcohol you want because there will be rivers of wine (Quran Surah 47:15). This contradiction still makes no sense to me. Along with abstaining from alcohol, pork or anything from a pig is forbidden. It seems that Islam borrowed that practice from the stricter Old Testament Jewish laws (in Leviticus 11:7-8).

"Forbidden to you (for food) are: dead meat, blood, the flesh of swine, and that on which hath been invoked the name of other than Allah"(Quran Surah 5:3).

This is a teaching that pertains not only to foods that are permissible or impermissible, but also in the laws pertaining to slaughtering, cooking and consuming foods. Even Muslims who are not devout will not eat pork. Others will extend the limitation to avoid eating gelatin or items made with pork by-products such as lecithin, lard (Ivory soap was a big no-no for us, as was Colgate toothpaste and marshmallows). It was surprising for us to see how many items contained pork by products. Foods that are cooked with alcohol for flavoring or as a marinade are forbidden. When I was growing up in the United States, the Imams would circulate updated lists that added forbidden foods and health products for Muslims. Today, there are lists available readily online for what is halal or haram.

Terms to know:
HARAM = not Kosher or forbidden
HALAL = Kosher or permissible

Hospitality

In a culture that thrives on community and family, hospitality is more than just serving food to others, it is a way of life. I grew up coming and going freely in between my neighbors' homes where the doors were always open and food was always shared - no matter how little they had. It is a culture of not just being gracious with their home, but also with food and time. You could stay as long as you wanted or could come in for a quick cup of hot tea.

There are some elderly Muslim women from Iran that I have had the privilege of knowing. Many of them live in modest retirement apartments and several have family abroad. One day, my daughter and a family friend went to deliver some treats for Easter. We came unannounced because we simply wanted to deliver the packages and leave. We should have remembered that there is no such thing as "simple." At almost every modest apartment, we were asked to come in for a cup of tea. Two of the women would not take "no" for an answer and when we insisted that we had several more to visit, one of them ran inside and brought out napkins with Turkish Delight for each one of us! It was a gesture as sweet as the candy! She told us that she couldn't bear to let us go without offering something from her home.

The gift of hospitality is inherent in the Muslim community and is reciprocated with gladness. It is practiced even here in the United States and I find it to be a sad state that many of my Muslim friends have not received invitations into Christian homes.

Gender Differences

While many Muslim women are fighting for equality, there are still very traditional roles held in great respect in the Muslim world. There are a few customs that Westerners don't realize about the Muslim male-female dynamic in public:

Speaking to the Male - In patriarchal societies, it is common to assume that the man is the head of the household. In the Middle East, this means that in doing business (even going to the store), the main person to speak with is the husband or father. The others will be ignored, including the wife, children or other family members. This may seem rude or inconsiderate in the West, but it is actually a sign of great deference to the head of the family. It should be noted that it's not always the elder gentleman in charge. In public, a devout Muslim woman will be accompanied by a mahram or a chaperone. A woman's mahram is anyone whom she is permanently forbidden to marry, because of blood ties, breastfeeding or ties through marriage, such as her father, son, or brother.[21] So the male can be a boy who may or may not have reached puberty.

Male to Male/Female to Female - A common mistake Christian missionaries make is to walk up and speak to anyone or even shake hands in greeting with either the male or female. This practice is not condoned in Muslim countries. Men should not speak to women who are not blood relatives - while touch is out of the question. There can be severe repercussions for them. Women (especially young

---

[21] "Fiqh of the Family. Mahram Relatives." (2012). https://islamqa.info/en/137095

women) absolutely should not speak to men they do not know. They will be seen as loose or worse, as prostitutes.

Old to Young - Again, there is a matter of respect in Muslim families. The elderly are highly regarded and should be greeted before the children. When speaking to a family, it is important to address the older person first. For women, it is not uncommon to call the older person "Auntie" and the men "Uncle" out of deference (not necessarily a familial relationship). It is considered impertinent and rude to address the older person with their first name. At the least, one should use "Mr." or "Mrs." for their name until they allow you to call them something else. Again, my husband was confused as to how many uncles and aunties I had until I told him that you can basically address anyone that way.

Convictions about the Quran

Prayers from the Quran (Taweez)

For a Muslim, the Quran is more than just a stack of pages with a beautiful binding. There is a strong belief in the book containing supernatural powers that Muslims attribute to the writings. Many will use verses from the Quran against evil spirits and will go as far as write the verse in ink on a piece of paper, place the paper in water, then drink the water to ward off spirits or to be healed. A woman wrote verses, placed them in a bathtub and bathed her child in the inky water to help him be healed.

I also subscribed to many of these beliefs when I was a Muslim. You would not find me without my Ayat al Kursi necklace (literal translation "Verse of the Chair" from Quran

2:255). This particular prayer is believed to make the walls of your house slick so that demons cannot enter it and angels will encamp around the area for protection. One time in college, I had taken it off for some reason and lost it. I was in an absolute panic until I found it again a week later.

The Imams (Holy Men) teach the following[22] about the entire chapter that contains the verses of the Ayat al Kursi, especially as it relates to the evil eye (which is a curse that anyone can arbitrarily put on you) and protection from jinn (demons). This chapter contains several of the verses and thus has importance, especially in dealing with the demonic Jinn:

1. Surah al-Faatiha: it is reported in Sahih Al-Bukhari and others that some Companions recited this on an afflicted person and he woke up with a start and walked away without feeling any more harm.

2. Al- Baqarah: it is reported in Sahih Muslim that the Prophet, said: *"Satan flees from the house where Soorat Al-Baqarah is being recited."*

3. The "two exorcists": which are Al-Falaq and Al-Naas: it is reported in Sunan Al-Tirmithi, Al-Nasaa'i and Ibn Majah that the Prophet sallallahu 'alayhi wa sallam, would supplicate to Allah against the Jinn and the evil eye until the *"two exorcists"* were revealed, and then he would seek refuge through them and abandoned the other chapters or verses he would use for seeking refuge. It is reported in Sunan Al-

---

[22] Fatwa (2004). [22] Fatwa (2004). Seeking to know the 'power' of the Qur'an and its verses Fatwa No. 88382
http://www.islamweb.net/emainpage/index.php?page=showfatwa&Option=Fatwal d&Id=88382

Tirmithi and Abu-Dawood that the Prophet, sallallahu 'alayhi wa sallam, said: *"Whoever recites the "two exorcists" in the morning and in the evening three times, it is enough for him (i.e., he will be protected from every evil)".*

It is reported in Sunan An-Nasaa'i that the Prophet, said: *"People cannot not seek refuge with anything better than Qul a'oothu bi Rabb'il falaq, and Qul a'oothu bi Rabb'in-naas."*
Verses:

1. The last two verses of Soorat Al-Baqarah: It is reported in Sahih-Al Bukhari, Muslim and others that the Prophet sallalahu 'alayhi wa sallam said about them: *"Whoever reads the last two verses of Soorat Al-Baqarah, he will be protected (from every evil)."*

2. Ayat Al-Kursi (the Verse of the Chair [Quran: 2:255]): The Prophet, sallallahu 'alayhi wa sallam, said: *"Whoever reads Ayat Al-Kursi, Satan will not come near to him."* (Al-Bukhari and Muslim).

As regards to bringing up the souls of the dead, nobody can do this. When the soul departs from the body, it goes to the Barzakh (the period after death until the Day of Judgment). The soul therein is either in enjoyment or being punished. People claiming to be able to bring up the souls of the dead are fallacious and untruthful. What they really do is call the Jinns, and this is a forbidden act which Allah has condemned in the Quran and those that do so are threatened with Hellfire; Allah says: {...*and their friends and helpers amongst men will say, "Our Lord, we benefited one from the other, but now we have reached our appointed term which You did appoint for us." He will say: "The Fire be your dwelling place; you*

will dwell therein forever, except as Allah may will. Certainly your Lord is All-Wise, All-Knowing.}
[from Hadith and Quran 6:128]

****

Quran's Status

Not only are the verses from the Quran held in high status as having mystical and magical power, but the same is attributed to the book itself. When a Muslim has a Quran in their house, they are to place it upon the highest shelf. When they open it to read, they have to recite a prayer and make sure that they have washed their hands and clean anything else that might touch it. When it is placed upon a table or a rug to read, the area needs to be wiped down. There are decorative wooden Quran stands available so the book will always be on a special holder and thus, a Muslim can avoid making a sinful error in handling the Quran. For my own Quran, my mother sewed a decorative satin fabric cover so that it would stay clean. This special consideration and care is also one of the reasons why Muslims get angry about people who wish to burn the Quran in protest. It is considered to be a great blasphemy against Allah.

✝ **CONNECTION:** When I first became a Christian, I was appalled! I saw Christians writing and highlighting in their Bible, throwing it casually underneath their seat in Sunday School and handling it recklessly while eating a cheeseburger. It was almost too much for me to bear! I did not understand why they disrespected their book so much.
I did not know that the Bible contains the teaching of Christ but that Christ Himself is the Word of God made flesh. In

Islam, the revelation of Allah is the book itself. In Christianity, the revelation of God is in the person of Christ.

You can help your Muslim friends make a connection to God's revelation by presenting them with a Bible. I have sewn decorative covers for the Bible I give to Muslims along with the explanation that we Christians do respect our Holy book. We believe it is the true, inerrant, Holy Spirit inspired word of God and that it is the best gift we could ever give another person. If there is hesitation from your friend, you can gently remind them that the Quran advocates belief in all of God's books. For my own use, I have several Bibles. I use one to write notes on and draw and then I have another one I read that has NO writing in it. Even something this small can become a big stumbling block and a distractor for a Muslim person.

Kaaba & the Meteorite Stone

The Kaaba is the shrine where every Muslim must visit at least once during their lifetime. There are lengthy rituals and cleansings that need to be done even before the Muslim embarks on the pilgrimage to Mecca (called the *Hajj* - the fifth pillar). What many outside Islam may not know or realize is that there is a meteorite housed in one of the corners of the Kaaba. It is now encased in silver and Muslims need to kiss the black stone as they perform the Hajj. Umrah is a voluntary or lesser pilgrimage that can be done at any time, while Hajj is mandatory and needs to be done during specified times of the Islamic calendar. or voluntary Tawaaf means to go around the Kaaba or circumambulation.

I have included the complete passages here for the Hadith[23] that support this:

1.   The Black Stone was sent down by Allah to this earth from Paradise. It was narrated that Ibn 'Abbaas said: The Messenger of Allah (peace and blessings of Allah be upon him) said: "The Black Stone came down from Paradise."
(Narrated by al-Tirmidhi, 877; al-Nasaa'i, 2935. The hadeeth was classed as saheeh by al-Tirmidhi).

2.   The Stone was whiter than milk, but the sins of the sons of Adam made it black.
It was narrated that Ibn 'Abbaas said: The Messenger of Allah (peace and blessings of Allah be upon him) said: "When the Black Stone came down from Paradise, it was whiter than milk, but the sins of the sons of Adam made it black."
(Narrated by al-Tirmidhi, 877; Ahmad, 2792. Classed as saheeh by Ibn Khuzaymah, 4/219. Al-Haafiz ibn Hajar classed it as qawiy (strong) in Fath al-Baari, 3/462).

(a)   Al-Mubaarakfoori said in *al-Marqaah*: This means, the sins of the sons of Adam who touched the stone, caused it to turn black. The hadeeth should be taken at face value, because there is no reason not to, either narrated in a report or by virtue of common sense.
(Tuhfat al-Ahwadhi, 3/525)
(b)   Al-Haafiz ibn Hajar said: Some heretics tried to criticize this hadeeth by saying: How come the sins of the mushrikeen turned it black and the worship of the people of Tawheed did not make it white?

I answer by quoting what Ibn Qutaybah said: If Allah had willed, that would have happened. But Allah has caused it to be the case that black usually changes other colors and it's not itself changed, which is the opposite to what happens with white.

(c)   Al-Muhibb al-Tabari said: The fact that it is black is a lesson for those who have insight. If sins can have this effect on an inanimate rock, then the effect they have on the heart is greater.

See Fath al-Baari, 3/463

3.   The Black Stone will come forth on the Day of Resurrection and will testify in favor of those who touched it in truth.

It was narrated that Ibn 'Abbaas said: The Messenger of Allah (peace and blessings of Allah be upon him) said concerning the Stone: "By Allah, Allah will bring it forth on the Day of Resurrection, and it will have two eyes with which it will see and a tongue with which it will speak, and it will testify in favor of those who touched it in sincerity."

Narrated by al-Tirmidhi, 961; Ibn Maajah, 2944

This hadeeth was classed as hasan by al-Tirmidhi, and as qawiy by al-Haafiz ibn Hajar in *Fath al-Baari, 3/462*

4.   Touching, kissing or pointing to the Black Stone – this is the first thing to be done when starting Tawaaf, whether it is for Hajj or 'Umrah, or voluntary Tawaaf.

It was narrated from Jaabir ibn 'Abd-Allah (may Allah be pleased with him) that when the Messenger of Allah (peace and blessings of Allah be upon him) came to Makkaah,[Mecca] he came to the Black Stone and touched it, then he walked to the right of it and ran three times and walked four times [around the Ka'bah].

(narrated by Muslim, 1218).

5.   The Prophet (peace and blessings of Allah be upon him) kissed the Black Stone, and his ummah followed his lead in doing so.

It was narrated that 'Umar (may Allah be pleased with him) came to the Black Stone and kissed it, then he said: "I know that you are only a stone which can neither bring benefit nor cause harm. Were it not that I had seen the Prophet (peace and blessings of Allah be upon him) kiss you, I would not have kissed you."

(Narrated by al-Bukhaari, 1520; Muslim, 1720)

6.   If a person is unable to kiss the Stone, he should touch it with his hand or something else, then he can kiss the thing with which he touched it.

(a)   It was narrated that Naafi' said: I saw Ibn 'Umar touch the Stone with his hand then he kissed his hand. I said, I have never ceased to do this since I saw the Messenger of Allah (peace and blessings of Allah be upon him) do it.

(Narrated by Muslim, 1268)

(b)   It was narrated that Abu Tufayl (may Allah be pleased with him) said: I saw the Messenger of Allah (peace and blessings of Allah be upon him) performing Tawaaf around the House, touching the corner [where the Stone is] with a crooked staff which he had with him, then kissing the staff.

(Narrated by Muslim, 1275).

7.   If a person is unable to do the above, then he can point to it with his hand and say "Allaahu akbar".

It was narrated that Ibn 'Abbaas said: The Messenger of Allah (peace and blessings of Allah be upon him) performed Tawaaf on his camel, and every time he came to the corner

[where the Stone is] he would point to it and say "Allaahu akbar."
(Narrated by al-Bukhaari, 4987).

8.   Touching the Stone is one of the things by means of which Allah expiates for sins

It was narrated that Ibn 'Umar said: I heard the Messenger of Allah (peace and blessings of Allah be upon him) say: "Touching them both [the Black Stone and al-Rukn al-Yamani] is an expiation for sins."

(Narrated by al-Tirmidhi, 959. This hadeeth was classed as hasan by al-Tirmidhi and as saheeh by al-Haakim (1/664). Al-Dhahabi agreed with him).

It is not permissible for a Muslim to annoy other Muslims at the Stone by hitting or fighting. The Prophet (peace and blessings of Allah be upon him) told us that the Stone will testify in favor of those who touched it in sincerity, which is not the case when a person touches it by disturbing the slaves of Allah.

****

✝ CONNECTION: We do not believe in the power of any inanimate object but believe in the rock of our salvation-- Jesus. *""The LORD lives, and blessed be my rock, and exalted be my God, the rock of my salvation... (2 Samuel 22:47)."*

"... and all ate the same spiritual food, and all drank the same spiritual drink. For they drank from the spiritual Rock that followed them, and the Rock was Christ (1 Corinthians 10:3-4)."

Jesus Christ is the firm foundation upon which we stand. There is no meteorite or object that will remove sins as is stated in the Hadith above. In the Old Testament verse from Samuel (and in Psalms), God is referred to the rock. Jesus

Christ is God in the flesh and represents the solid foundation as the word of God for all who believe in Him.

Jinn

Muslims believe in mischievous spirits called Jinn. The word Jinn means "to hide" or "hidden." We get the English word "Genie" from the Arabic Jinn. They are one of my favorite topics to speak about because they are considered a mystery even to the Muslim people and have a host of traditions that encompass them. Belief in Jinn is part of Muslim superstition and is easily influenced by the different countries' culture as well. Jinn are considered to be half human and half fire, part of the creation with a body and a soul, and only Allah has power over them. Therefore, Muslims recite aloud the Quran as incantations to ward off the evil spirits. There is an entire chapter in the Quran titled "Al Jinn" in Surah 72. There are thousands of disturbing blog posts online where Muslims chat openly about how the Jinn are giving them troubles - from missing socks in the dryer to demonic possession of themselves or family members.

✝ **CONNECTION:** Offer to pray for your Muslim friend in the name of Jesus by explaining that ONLY Jesus has the power over demonic spirits (Quran states that 'Isa was given the ability to cure the blind and the lepers, and to bring the dead back to life). The Holy Spirit can break through spiritual strongholds for those who call upon the Lord Jesus as Savior (Luke 10:17).

The Holy Spirit indwells all who are children of God, so we need not fear becoming demon-possessed ourselves (1

Corinthians 3:16; 1 John 4:4; Romans 8:9–15, 38–39). We have the sword of the Spirit (Ephesians 6:17), which is the word of God. We are given such great confidence and we bring light into dark places because of who we serve!

Dogs & the Unclean

The previous section discussed Haram and Halal food for Muslims. The idea of Haram and Halal doesn't only apply to food, but also to other things such as actions of a Muslim and items in the home.

Dogs do not escape this judgment from Islam. They are considered to be unclean animals and the prophet forbade them from being in the house. In fact, when I was growing up, we were told that angels would never visit the house of a person who had a dog, thus we were allowed to have a guard dog that lived outside but we were never allowed to even touch him.

The information about dogs is not in the Quran, but there are various Hadith that address this topic:

1. I heard Allah's Apostle(P.B.U.H) saying; "Angels (of Mercy) do not enter a house wherein there is a dog or a picture of a living creature (a human being or an animal)" (Hadith – Bukhari 3:515).
2. That the Messenger of Allah said: "Whoever acquires a dog – with the exception of a dog to guard livestock, a hunting dog, or a farm dog – each day a Qirat (a unit of measurement) is deducted from his reward. (Abu Dawood - Narrated Abu Hurairah. Sunan Abu Dawood Book 16 Hadith 2838).

The saliva of the dog is extremely naajis (Haram), because the Prophet (peace and blessings of Allah be upon him) said: "If a dog licks the vessel of any one of you, let him throw away whatever was in it and wash it seven times (reported by Hadith Sahih Muslim, no. 418).

In a country where people think of their pets as extended family or even as their "furry children," this might be a tough concept. I recall the events of one particular evening, when my family was invited to dinner at a person's home. We had a pleasant meal and the host's dogs remained outside so they would not disturb us during our visit. After dinner, they let the dogs inside so they could be fed. As they were rinsing off the dishes and loading them into the dishwasher, the American husband called one of the dogs over and allowed him to lick the plate clean. Needless to say, my entire family was disgusted by the action and it took months of convincing to even get my parents to go visit our friends again. They went, but politely declined to eat at their home.

✝ **CONNECTION:** Please put your dogs away when you invite a Muslim over to your home as a sign of respect for them! We do not want to create any more stumbling blocks than those already present. It is a little courtesy that goes a long way.

Amulets & Talismans

While there is evidence of many cultures that incorporate and use everyday objects as superstitious charms to ward off evil, in Islam there is an undercurrent that is not talked about outside the community. Each country has its own cultural influence, so this is not an exhaustive list, but merely a few examples of the ones I knew about. In the Southeast Asian countries, there is a widespread use of talismans and amulets - from the verses of the Quran to other objects that have been prayed over. Some of these include:

Evil Eye - Usually in all blue colors, sometimes with a Hamsa Hand (idea that it is the divine hand of God), used to keep away the eyes and curses of evil from others. It is common to see the evil eye amulet placed near the doorways of the home or dangling from a car's rearview mirror. Many are fashioned into jewelry. There is Hadith that told about Muhammad attributing one third of deaths ("those in the grave") were there due to the curse of the evil eye and warned people to do ritual washings to wash off the curse.

Muslims believe this verse about the evil eye of jealousy from the Quran (113:1,5): "Say, I seek refuge in the Lord of Daybreak...And from the evil of the envier when he envieth."

786 - This is a belief that was shared with me during final exam time when I was a student in Pakistan. The numbers 786 are supposed to represent the Quranic expression "Bismillah al-Rahman al-Rahim". Some believe that if you add up the numbers of the letters, it will add up to 786, etc. It then becomes a lucky number, a charm or even something to bring good luck on an exam. This is not something supported by the Quran or Hadith.

Along with the numbers, there are also five Arabic letters (*kaf ha ya ayn sadd*) which appear at the beginning of certain chapters in the Quran. These single letters are some of the 'mysterious letters of the Qur'an' which show up on 29 of the 114 chapters. Some Muslims believe that these have magical power to guard Muslims and thus can often be found engraved on amulets or beautifully captured by artful calligraphy.

The name of Muhammad can also be written down and worn as a charm. I had another gold locket my parents brought back from Pakistan for me that looked like a tiny Quran, with the name of Muhammad engraved on one side and Allah on the other. I also wore this locket for my identity as a Muslim and to ward off evil.

Taweez - As mentioned previously, there is a great reliance on writing down verses and prayers from the Quran to wear on the person's body in hopes that it will ward off evil or allow them to be healed. There are special vials, necklaces and other objects made to wear, carry or place in the home. Also, it is permissible to write or say prayers out loud and blow them on the individual as well. When I was sick, my nanny used to say prayers and blow them on my face to ward off evil spirits or any evil eye that may have been causing the sickness. Even though I considered myself to be an educated American woman, I believed this to be true and often repeated this ritual with my own children as well.

Hadith Beliefs

There are a lot of beliefs to consider from the Hadith. I am sharing just a few as they might be worth exploring from the Western view. Many find these to be absolutely incredulous, however, it is important to note that many (not all!) Muslims take these seriously as warnings to live their lives the best way possible for Allah.

Satan causes yawning (Bukhari 73:245).

Spoons should be covered before going to bed (Bukhari 69:527).

Oversleeping is caused by Satan urinating in one's ear (Bukhari 54:492).

The bathroom - and some say any room -should be entered with the left foot first (Fiqh – Islamic law).

Keeping a dog as a pet will cost the owner a celestial reward (Bukhari 67:389).

A man should spit only to his left (Muslim 71:49).

A person should wipe their bottom with an odd number of stones after defecating (Bukhari 4:163).

Satan sleeps in one's nose, so water should be snorted vigorously each morning (Bukhari 54:516).

Cursed is the lady who wears false hair (Bukhari 60:409).

Bad dreams can be warded off by spitting three times over the left side of the bed (Bukhari 87:115).

The right shoe should be put on before the left (Muslim 514).

No one should enter the house through the back door (Quran 2:189).

Muslims should be buried facing toward Mecca (Sharia-Islamic law).

✝ **CONNECTION:** Christians may also have misunderstandings of Scripture, traditions and superstitions. The difference here is that these are NOT taught by JESUS or the Bible. Muslims will bring up Old Testament practices that are not performed today and that are not prescribed behavior for us (i.e. Leviticus 14 – cleansing from different activities/sickness or as mentioned before, the eating of pork or other unclean animals).

Some of my Catholic friends add extra biblical teaching with superstition claims such as having items blessed by a priest for special reasons and following traditions such as burying St. Joseph upside down in their front yard to help their home sell quickly. Protestants do not follow these traditions but I know of several people who wear special verses as charms to combat anxiety or bring them good luck. There is also another phenomenon I have personally witnessed called the "Lucky Dip." This is where a well-meaning Christian will close their eyes and flip to a place in the Bible, expecting to have a special message waiting from the Lord for them. Please know that these are not things we should do as

Christians for our hope and our all-in-all is Jesus Christ. Prayer is more than sufficient, for we have the Holy Spirit of God living within us!

Ways to Connect our Muslim friends to the Gospel message:

JESUS conquers ALL:
Power over demonic spirits
Power to cleanse us from sin
Power to destroy Satan the enemy
Power over SIN & DEATH!

1. Muslims pray before eating, driving, starting anything.
   TRUE OR FALSE

2. Jinn are:

   _____.

3. The Left Hand is _____ and used for _____
   while the Right is _____ and used for
   _____.

4. Having dogs in a Muslim home means _____ will
   not visit.

5. The physical book of the Quran is _____.

6. The Muslim will place their Quran on the _____
   _____ in the house.

7. The Kaaba has a _____ _____ that must be
   kissed during Hajj. It turned from a _____ color to a
   _____ color due to _____.

APPLICATION

What are 3 things you learned about ISLAM in this chapter?

_____

_____

_____

How can you help a non-believer understand rituals and superstitions when compared to Christ's power?

_____

_____

_____

How can you connect the information from this chapter into a presentation of the Gospel?

_____

_____

_____

Chapter 4

Women in Islam

There is neither Jew nor Greek, there is neither slave nor free, there is no male and female, for you are all one in Christ Jesus.

Galatians 3:28

But the woman, knowing what had happened to her, came in fear and trembling and fell down before him and told him the whole truth. And he said to her, "Daughter, your faith has made you well; go in peace, and be healed of your disease."

Mark 5:33-34

Surah An Nisa – The Women

This chapter in the Quran is written mainly for men and contains instructions on how to marry, rules on inheritance for men and women (they only receive half portion after the men in the family get their full portions), divorce, children and also female slaves. My parents are highly educated, progressive and with three daughters, they have always held a higher view of women's rights than those found in many Islamic nations. Growing up, I was never acquainted with this chapter nor did I know the information it contained. My father always treated his wife and daughters with love and kindness.

There are several passages that are disturbing, including calling women "weak-minded" in Surah 4:5. The Quran also does not specify what is a "marriageable age" (Surah 4:6 & 65:4). Muhammad entered into marriage with Aisha, daughter of his close friend and companion when she was age 6 and he was 50. The marriage was then consummated three years later when she was 9 and he was 53 according to Ibn Hisham. While many Muslim men do not seek out child brides, the example is set for the Muslim world to follow in the footsteps of their prophet Muhammad. It is absolutely permissible for grown men to marry children in Muslim countries.

The Quran allows a man to readily replace one wife with another (Surah an Nisa 4:20) and the same chapter allows men to marry women already married (captive slaves), which is again what Muhammad did several times during his campaigns of war. There are also rules in the chapter about marriage and divorce, to allow polygamy (Surah an Nisa 4:3 allows up to four wives, even though Muhammad had approximately 11 to 13 wives and concubines).

Women are worth half of a man - from inheritance to their testimony in court of law (Surah an Nisa 4:11). A husband is allowed to beat his wife or wives if he sees fit (Surah an Nisa 4:34). Of course, one cannot forget about the houris (also called "Hoor" and "al-hoor a-'iyn" which are fair, doe-eyed, buxom women) promised by Allah to Muslim men in Paradise. These are supernatural women who remain eternal virgins for the men's sexual pleasure.

"Therein (Gardens) will be Khayraatun-Hisaan [fair (wives) good and beautiful];

Then which of the Blessings of your Lord will you both (jinn
and men) deny?
Hoor (beautiful, fair females) guarded in pavilions;
Then which of the Blessings of your Lord will you both (jinn
and men) deny?
With whom no man or jinni has had Tamth [opening their
hymens with sexual intercourse] before them.
Then which of the Blessings of your Lord will you both (jinn
and men) deny?
Reclining on green cushions and rich beautiful mattresses"
(Surah al-Rahmaan 55:70-76).
"And (there will be) Hoor (fair females) with wide lovely
eyes (as wives for Al-Muttaqoon – the pious). Like unto
preserved pearls" (Surah al-Waaqi'ah 56:22-23).

There is hot debate in the media and on websites that the
number 72 for the virgins is a myth. Some Muslims will
deny this belief altogether out of ignorance, for the Quran
mentions this in Hadith 2687 and gives the number 72 for
the virgins in Paradise.

"It was reported in the hadeeth of al-Miqdaam ibn Ma'di
Karb that the Prophet (peace and blessings of Allah be upon
him) said:
"The martyr (shaheed) has seven blessings from Allah: he is
forgiven from the moment his blood is first shed; he will be
shown his place in Paradise; he will be spared the trial of the
grave; and he will be secure on the Day of the Greatest
Terror (the Day of Judgment); there will be placed on his
head a crown of dignity, one ruby of which is better than
this world and all that is in it; **he will be married to seventy-
two of al-hoor al-'iyn**; and he will be permitted to intercede
for seventy of his relatives." According to another report, the

martyr has six blessings from Allah. According to other reports (the number is) six, or nine, or ten.
(Narrated by al-Tirmidhi, who said it is a hasan hadeeth. Also narrated by Ibn Maajah in al-Sunan, by Ahmad, by 'Abd al-Razzaaq in al-Musannaf, by al-Tabaraani in al-Kabeer, and by Sa'eed ibn Mansoor in al-Sunan).
from; The six blessings of the martyrs"
(Shaykh Waleed al-Firyaan, Islam Q&A, Fatwa No. 8511).

While the information about the forgiveness of sins for martyrs combined with infinite sexual pleasure with concubines and eternal virgins can be troubling for many (and rightly so!), there is a bright side. Mary is held in high regard as one being pious and doing what Allah bid her to do. There is only **one** woman named in the entire Quran. Not even Muhammad's favored wife is named. It is Maryam, or Mary - Jesus Christ's mother. There is an entire chapter (Surah 19 - Maryam) devoted to Jesus (named Isa [pronounced "ee-saw"] in Arabic- taken presumably from the Greek "Iesous").

As a Muslim, this was the first time I had ever read anything about the life of Jesus. HOWEVER, they do not see Jesus as the Son of God. The Quran states:

"They say, " Allah has taken a son." Exalted is He! Rather, to Him belongs whatever is in the heavens and the earth. All are devoutly obedient to Him, Originator of the heavens and the earth. When He decrees a matter, He only says to it, "Be," and it is (Surah al Baqarah 2:116-117)."

Muslims know generalities about Isa but are not encouraged to learn about Him, while Abraham and other prophets are a part of normal conversation and even daily prayer recitations for Muslims. Many Sunni Muslims believe that "one who sits on the right hand of God will come to judge" on judgment day is Isa Masih - Jesus the Messiah!

"(And he shall be a sign for (the coming of) the Hour)
means, sign and "One of the signs of the Hour will be the appearance of `Isa son of Maryam before the Day of Resurrection." Something similar was also narrated from Abu Hurayrah, Ibn `Abbas, `Abu Al-`Aliyah, Abu Malik, `Ikrimah, Al-Hasan, Qatadah, Ad-Dahhak and others. Many Mutawatir Hadiths report that the Messenger of Allah said that **`Isa will descend before the Day of Resurrection as a just ruler and fair judge**. (*Tafsir Ibn Kathir*[24])."

One of the most troublesome aspects for me as a former Muslim was the fact that women are considered unclean when menstruating or bleeding from childbirth and are not allowed to pray, fast or be touched by a man. This is yet another parallel to the Levitical laws of Judaism. The problem here is that a woman is in a perpetual state of being spiritually inferior to men. She will have to live a lifetime of trying to make up her prayers and good works.

In the Bible, Jesus interacts with several women. He never rebukes them nor does he take them on as multiple wives. In each instance, He treats them with greater dignity and respect than what the Jews at the time showed women. Our Lord's tenderness was shown to me at a personal level through a particular passage in Matthew 19:20-22:

---

[24]Tafsir Ibn Kathir.
http://www.qtafsir.com/index.php?option=com_content&task=view&id=2076&Ite
mid=99

"Suddenly a woman who had suffered from bleeding for twelve years came up behind Him and touched the fringe of His cloak. She said to herself, "If only I touch His cloak, I will be healed."Jesus turned and saw her. "Take courage, daughter," He said, "your faith has healed you." And the woman was cured from that very hour."

I read these verses for the very first time only months after I had become a Christian believer. I was absolutely undone by the power I saw in these words. They revealed Jesus to me in such a beautiful and poignant way. He was a rabbi - a holy man of God. Touching a woman who was bleeding would have made Him unclean for His own prayer and worship. Instead of sharp, swift degradation and humiliation for breaking a social rule, he gave back her dignity and publicly, lovingly called her "daughter." He not only physically restored her, but also provided her spiritual restoration. As a former Muslim woman, I had faced the degradation of being an unclean woman in front of Allah, whom I was desperately trying to please. Here, God Himself in flesh raises her up ,makes her whole and tenderly calls her his "daughter."

✝ **CONNECTION:** Women make up half of the Muslim world! Many are hidden behind their husbands, fathers or behind a veil that covers them both physically and spiritually. Due to the cultural and religious boundaries (imposed by Sharia law in some places including Europe), women should witness to women and men to men. Women have a unique opportunity to go into the home, build and invest in a relationship with a Muslim woman, learn customs, share recipes, compare life's trials and bounce babies on their knees. When we give the gift of time and hospitality to others, we receive the privilege of having a profound insight into the lives of Muslim women. There, one can find that they are truly not that different from us as Christians. When I was a Muslim, I had an intense love for my family and my children - just as I do now. The home was a special source of pride for me.

It is a unique blessing to be able to pray for your Muslim friend and to see the Lord work in her and her family's life. Watching hearts incline towards the word of God through honest and open discussions is truly gratifying. I encourage you to get to know all the women the Lord has placed around you - Muslim and non-Muslim. Do you know your neighbors? When is the last time you touched base with a friend who is a non-believer? There is a deep-seated yearning for women to socialize and for us to connect as human beings and later, God willing, as sisters in Christ.

1. Women in Islam cannot _____ or _____ when bleeding.

2. Women in Islam are to be given _____ the inheritance of a male.

3. _____ is the only woman mentioned by name in the entire Quran.

4. Heaven is called _____ in the Quran and differs from the Bible.

5. Men can have multiple wives on earth and in _____.

6. There is no minimum age for girls to marry in Islam.
   TRUE OR FALSE

APPLICATION

What are 3 things you learned about women in ISLAM vs Christianity in this chapter?

_____

_____

_____

Who are the women in your life that you should be praying for regularly?

_____

_____

_____

How will you share the Gospel with other women?

_____

_____

Chapter 5

Understanding Assumptions

Beloved, do not believe every spirit, but test the spirits to see whether they are from God, for many false prophets have gone out into the world.

1 John 4:1

Be Educated

All Arabs are Muslim or All Muslims are Arab

There are many assumptions made about Islam. One of the first is that all Arabs are Muslims. This is something that I believed when I was a Muslim even when I lived in the Middle East! Because the religion started in the Middle East, it's identity is set with Arabia. The fact of the matter is that around 80-84%[25] of Muslims are Arab or have Arabic as their native language. Muslims have a great diversity as they live all over the world and some of the largest Muslim nations are found in Southeast Asia and Africa.

There should also be caution in the way Christians explain terms. When I first became a Christian, almost all Christian

---

[25] "Demographics of Islam." Berkley Center.
https://berkleycenter.georgetown.edu/essays/demographics-of-islam

terminology was new to me. I did not understand the words, even though I had lived in the United States for 25 years. I did not understand what "grace" was because there is no grace offered to sinners in Islam. Allah may offer mercy and compassion, but there is no grace.

Trinity

The term "Trinity" is also a source for confusion. Muslims believe that the Christian's Trinity is God, Jesus and Mary. Why would a Muslim believe this? It's in the Quran:
"O People of the Scripture, do not commit excess in your religion or say about Allah except the truth. The Messiah, Jesus, the son of Mary, was but a messenger of Allah and His word which He directed to Mary and a soul [created at a command] from Him. So believe in Allah and His messengers. And do not say, "Three"; desist - it is better for you. Indeed, Allah is but one God. Exalted is He above having a son. To Him belongs whatever is in the heavens and whatever is on the earth. And sufficient is Allah as Disposer of affairs (Surah an Nisa 4:171)."

"They have certainly disbelieved who say, " Allah is the third of three." And there is no god except one God. And if they do not desist from what they are saying, there will surely afflict the disbelievers among them a painful punishment (Surah al Maida 5:73)."

"And [beware the Day] when Allah will say, "O Jesus, Son of Mary, did you say to the people, **'Take me and my mother as deities besides Allah ?'**" He will say, "Exalted are You! It was not for me to say that to which I have no right. If I had said it, You would have known it. You know what is within myself, and I do not know what is within Yourself. Indeed, it is You who is Knower of the unseen (Surah al Maidah 5:116)."

While the Quran does not come out and call the relationships of Allah, Isa, and Maryam a Trinity, there is implication from these verses that the followers of Jesus are polytheists who have taken on two other gods to worship besides Allah. Furthermore, the resurrection of Christ is denied, for the crucifixion was denied in the Quran. There is also confusion on the spirit of Allah and the Quran even names the spirit, Gabriel.

Islam means Peace

Another assumption is that the word Islam means "peace." Islam does not mean peace, it means "to submit," namely to the will of Allah as it is revealed to Muhammad in the Quran. In the media, there is a concerted effort towards redefining of the word Islam. Muslim Imams and Clerics are stating publicly that the word Islam comes from the root word "silm" or "salam" that means peace. This is not true and even Muslims will tell you this is not true from statements in the Quran.

I personally think that this notion might be an effort to bring about less fear in the minds of those who erroneously think that all Muslims are terrorists. There is a political movement to spin the idea of Islam as a peaceful religion in order to comfort those in the West who do not know Islamic teachings especially after the September 11, 2001 terrorist attacks. In spite of these efforts, one simply has to turn to the Muslims' own book:

"[Remember, O believers], when Allah promised you one of the two groups - that it would be yours - and you wished that the unarmed one would be yours. But Allah intended to establish the truth by His words and to eliminate the disbelievers (Surah 8:7)."

"Indeed, the penalty for those who wage war against Allah and His Messenger and strive upon earth [to cause] corruption is none but that they be killed or crucified or that their hands and feet be cut off from opposite sides or that they be exiled from the land. That is for them a disgrace in this world; and for them in the Hereafter is a great punishment (Surah 5:33)."

It is difficult to find peace within the Quran for those who do not subscribe to Muhammad's plan. Peace could come, but only if you submit to the will of Allah as dictated in the Quran. This was my issue as well. The more I tried to read and follow what the Quran said, the less peace I felt in my soul.

Quran is the Word of God

For Christians, the Word of God is Jesus. "In the beginning was the Word, and the Word was with God, and the Word was God. He was in the beginning with God. All things were made through him, and without him was not any thing made that was made." (John 1:1-3). In Islam, the word of God is a physical book. When speaking with Muslims, it is important not to insult the Quran or treat it negatively. They do not understand the revelation of God through Jesus as Christians do and that is our commission in sharing the Gospel.

Teachings

In Islam, the strongest teaching and the pivotal principle is the *Tawhid* (or Tawheed) which is an Arabic word for the "oneness of God." The Oxford Islamic Studies website states: "Tawhid is the defining doctrine of Islam. It declares absolute monotheism—the unity and uniqueness of God as creator and sustainer of the universe. Used by Islamic reformers and activists as an organizing principle for human society and the basis of religious knowledge, history, metaphysics, aesthetics, and ethics, as well as social, economic, and world order."[26]

This is the fundamental concept that unites all of Islam and makes the claim that Christians are polytheists even more glaring to other Muslims. Due to the imagery that exists in many churches (statues, icons, paintings), Muslims assume that Christians worship both Jesus and Mary as idols. Again, this is considered blasphemy (called *"Shirk"*) and an affront to the Tawhid. There are many who claim that Christians worship 1+1+1 = 3   It can also mathematically be explained that we worship 1 God in 3 persons, better expressed by 1x1x1=1 (or 1^3).

Not

1+1+1=1

but

$$1^3 = 1 \times 1 \times 1$$

Denial of the Crucifixion

When I share my testimony, I explain another frequently asked question: "Do Christians and Muslims worship the same God?"

[26]"Esposito, John (editor). Tawhid." In *The Oxford Dictionary of Islam. Oxford Islamic Studies Online*. 08-Jun-2018.
http://www.oxfordislamicstudies.com/article/opr/t125/e2356.

When I first became a Christian, I would have answered yes. I did not understand the Trinity and also did not understand fully who Jesus was or who He claimed He was. I had accepted Jesus as Lord based on what I had read in the Quran and what I heard when the Gospel was first shared with me. I did not know anything more than who I prayed to (Allah) and that Allah pointed me straight to Christ. Again, I had no idea who the Holy Spirit was or even that He existed!

Today, when I am asked the question, my answer is based upon what I know in the Quran and the Bible. The Quran absolutely denies the crucifixion because it was a shameful way to die even in 7th century Arabia. Since Allah would not allow this to happen to bring shame to one of his prophets, Jesus didn't die. Islam teaches that Jesus was simply removed off the cross and either Judas or an angel was crucified to death in his place.

If there is no crucifixion, there is no atonement for sins by the shedding of Jesus Christ's blood on the cross. If there is no atonement, there is no Savior. If Jesus did not die, there is no Resurrection. If there was no Resurrection, there is no ascension or coming of the Holy Spirit. If there is no Holy Spirit, there is no Trinity or Triune God.

No... we do not worship the same God. Christians worship GOD Almighty. God in three persons, blessed Trinity.

"Now if Christ is proclaimed as raised from the dead, how can some of you say that there is no resurrection of the dead? But if there is no resurrection of the dead, then not even Christ has been raised. And if Christ has not been raised, then our preaching is in vain and your faith is in vain. We are even found to be misrepresenting God, because we testified about God that he raised Christ, whom he did not raise if it

is true that the dead are not raised. For if the dead are not raised, not even Christ has been raised. And if Christ has not been raised, your faith is futile and you are still in your sins. Then those also who have fallen asleep in Christ have perished. If in Christ we have hope in this life only, we are of all people most to be pitied.
But in fact Christ has been raised from the dead, the firstfruits of those who have fallen asleep."

1 Corinthians 15:12-20

Sin

The concept of sin in Islam is yet another place of difference, since Muslims do not believe in "Original Sin." They believe that babies are born sinless and are a clean slate upon which their good and bad deeds are written. Therefore, "sin" becomes the equivalent of "bad deeds" and not an affront against the holiness of God Almighty. The Quran teaches that Adam sinned and so did the rest of the prophets including Muhammad who asked Allah to forgive his sins. Muslims see Allah as a good businessman who has scales to weigh their good and bad works. All Muslims can do good works to help them get to Paradise. However, there is nothing that tells them how much each bad work is worth. For example, when I was little, I asked my parents if lying to them was worth more in bad works than lying to someone else in the family or friends. Doing bad deeds to infidels does not figure into the good or bad works equation. Lying to infidels is considered to be a non-issue for Muslims and there is even a word for it called Taqiyya[27].

The Quran identifies Muhammad as sinful (Surah 40:55, 48:2, and 47:19) and there are several Hadith that state that he even

[27] Ibrahim, R (2008)"Islam's Doctrines of Deception." Middle East Forum.
https://www.meforum.org/articles/2009/islam-s-doctrines-of-deception

prayed for Allah's forgiveness (Sahih Muslim, [10], Book 4, Number 1212). Below are the verses from the Quran:

"Therefore have patience; God's promise is surely true. Implore forgiveness for your sins, and celebrate the praise of your Lord evening and morning (Surah 40:55)."

"Indeed, We have given you, [O Muhammad], a clear conquest so that God may forgive you your past and future sins, and perfect His goodness to you. And [that] Allah may aid you with a mighty victory (Surah 48:1-3)."

"So know, [O Muhammad], that there is no deity except Allah and ask forgiveness for your sin and for the believing men and believing women. And Allah knows of your movement and your resting place (Surah 47:19)."

The Quran says ONLY one man is sinless: Jesus. He is called "pure" (or zakiyya in Arabic) in Surah 19:19. He was pure from birth and remained pure. It is also mentioned in the Hadith Book 43, 193[28]. The Bible affirms Jesus had no sin:

"You know that he appeared in order to take away sins, and in him there is no sin (1 John 3:5)."

"He committed no sin, neither was deceit found in his mouth. When he was reviled, he did not revile in return; when he suffered, he did not threaten, but continued entrusting himself to him who judges justly (1 Peter 2:22-3)."

Judgment Day

While Muslims believe in Judgment Day, they believe that all will be judged and it is every man for himself. They do not believe in a Savior, since they are responsible for their own salvation through good works that will help them get to

---

[28] Sahih Muslim. The Book of Virtues. https://sunnah.com/muslim/43/193

Paradise. There is no way for a Muslim person to know how many good works or bad works they have. If they die while in the act of doing something bad, they have no way to pay that off. They also have no way of knowing which way the scales will tip or even if they stay balanced at an equal good works to bad works ratio. There is no assurance of Salvation. There is no Savior and there is no understanding of what they might need to be saved from.

Honor/Shame

Muslims live and thrive in a community. The Arab culture and history is based upon the nomadic Bedouins who traveled together. There is great emphasis placed on genealogy, heredity and group identity. This is not just a Muslim observation, but one that is true for most Eastern cultures. The book of Matthew starts off with a long list of names in the genealogy of Jesus Christ. I know many Christians find this to be long and dull. I found it fascinating and quite impressive that Matthew was able to trace Jesus Christ's roots all the way back!

This is the kind of thing that Muslims favor and desire. The spirit of the West, especially the American value of individualism is as foreign to the cultures of the East as their cultures are to the West. Their strong group and cultural identity cause great alarm for the Muslim community. When one Muslim is threatened or blasphemed, it is as though all have been insulted. This is the case of Charlie Hebdo[29]. He was the artist in France who made cartoons of Muhammad. He did several things that caused a riot and ultimately cost him his life.

---

[29] CNN.com Dec. 25, 2017. 2015 Charlie Hebdo Attacks Fast Facts
https://www.cnn.com/2015/01/21/europe/2015-paris-terror-attacks-fast-facts/index.html

He made a graven image of the Muslim prophet. He insulted Islam. He insulted every single Muslim person in the world.

There is a great deal of energy spent in protecting both the relationships and reputations of Muslims. The community, called the Ummah, sees itself as policing those who fall away from the tenets of Islam or even the traditions of the religion (for example, not showing up often to the Friday prayer at the local mosque or to the religious events). When I was a rebellious teenager, I was told by some of the mothers in the community that they would not hesitate to call my parents to report on what I was doing or how I had misbehaved. That threat alone was more than enough to help keep me walking on a relatively straight and narrow.

Because of the relationship ties, the Muslim community focuses on the family. They do not condone divorce publicly so they seem to present a solidified front, especially to the outsiders in the West. Loyalty comes first to Islam, then family, then to the community. It is okay to bend the rules or to lie in order to save face. It is okay to do these things especially if it makes Islam look good to the outside world.

This is one of the reasons why a Muslim will hesitate to even talk about Jesus with a Christian! If someone else saw or heard them discussing Christianity, because others around them might think that they are forsaking Islam to become a Christian. A rejection of Islam carries with it a great loss of community, culture, being disowned by your family and in some cases, even a change of your name. Muslims believe that because many change their name to Arabic names when they become Muslim (like Cassius Clay to Muhammad Ali), that the same is true for when they become Christian. My mother thought that about me when I had accepted Christ. She was worried I would change my given name - I did not, for my identity is not in my name, it is in Christ.

✝ **CONNECTION:** Adam is considered to be a prophet in Islam (Who did he prophesize to? Eve?). He is not considered to be the one to bring sin and death into the world as we see in the book of Genesis. We can help to make a connection to the events that took place in the Garden of Eden with the first Adam to the events in the Garden of Gethsemane with the last Adam, Jesus.

The body of Christ in community can also be a beautiful way to minister to Muslims. When they accept Christ, they stand to lose a lot. I was disowned by my parents, my sisters, extended family and friends. I was told that people in my community would come find me and kill me for turning my back on Islam. These apostates are considered to be the worst kind of sinners in Islam and their punishment is death. This is a real threat as it is stated in the Quran and Hadith several times as a means of action for Muslims to take even today- it would be considered Jihad:

"Whoever changes his Islamic religion, kill him" (Sahih Bukhari 84:57)"

"And when the sacred months have passed, then kill the polytheists wherever you find them and capture them and besiege them and sit in wait for them at every place of ambush. But if they should repent, establish prayer, and give zakah, let them [go] on their way. Indeed, Allah is Forgiving and Merciful (Surah at Tawbah 9:5)."

"[Remember] when your Lord inspired to the angels, "I am with you, so strengthen those who have believed. I will cast terror into the hearts of those who disbelieved, so strike [them] upon the necks and strike from them every fingertip."(Surah al Anfal 8:12)."

Witnessing to a Muslim one-on-one can be more effective than witnessing to them in a group. They will be more prone to defer to the group than to the message an outsider brings them (yet, I know that the Holy Spirit can and will move in a group!). We can address also the understanding of shame and honor through the invitation of hosting and honoring a Muslim guest at a meal. When we invite our Muslim friends, we prepare a seat at the table for them and try to host them with the best we have. The connection of honor goes further than that. We can share with them the honor God Almighty gives us through Christ - that we can approach the throne of God boldly as His adopted children and we share in Christ's glory!

"For you did not receive the spirit of slavery to fall back into fear, but you have received the Spirit of adoption as sons, by whom we cry, "Abba! Father!" The Spirit himself bears witness with our spirit that we are children of God, and if children, then heirs—heirs of God and fellow heirs with Christ, provided we suffer with him in order that we may also be glorified with him. (Romans 8:15-17)."

We can also ask the question "Why would God "condescend" to be shamed and humiliated on the Cross?"

TRINITY:
Christians _____, _____, & _____
Muslims _____, _____, & _____

ISLAM:
People think Islam means _____, but it means _____.

One who practices Islam is called a _____.
Quran vs. Christ = _____ vs. _____.

TEACHINGS
*Allah is _____. He has no _____ or _____.
*Shirk:_____.
*Tawhid means: _____ _____ of _____ _____
Do Christians and Muslims worship the same God?
TRUE OR FALSE

SIN
Quran calls only 1 person sinless or pure and that person is _____.

Muslims believe their _____ _____ can get them to Paradise.
Instead of using the word "sin," we can use the words _____ deeds & _____ deeds.

APPLICATION

What are 2 things you learned about the Trinity and Christ in this chapter:

_____

_____

What did you learn about the Honor/Shame culture?

_____

_____

Why would God "condescend" to be humiliated on the cross?

_____

_____

_____

How will you connect this information to the Gospel?

_____

_____

_____

Chapter 6

Reaching Muslims Through Evangelism

How then will they call on him in whom they have not believed? And how are they to believe in him of whom they have never heard? And how are they to hear without someone preaching? And how are they to preach unless they are sent? As it is written, "How beautiful are the feet of those who preach the good news!"

Romans 10:14-15

When one is born in a Muslim country, they are not given a choice to declare their religion. The person is automatically considered to be a Muslim. This is absolutely the case for all who are born to Muslim parents. Children are not allowed to pick and choose what religion they will be. There is no decision to make.

As a former Muslim, I was no different in my view. I saw the United States as a Christian nation. Not just a nation that had Christian roots but actually as a nation in which everyone American was a Christian. The term "everyone" includes all in Hollywood and the immoral behavior of the entertainment industry. This is a huge obstacle to overcome, as many Muslims have never met a bona fide Christian who has shared the Gospel of Jesus Christ with them.

I have met Christians who would love to share the Gospel with Muslims but the desire is mixed with fear and hope. My leader Paula from Bible Study Fellowship (BSF) reminds us several times a year that:

Fear & Faith cannot exist together.
One will drive out the other.

There are concrete ways to overcome the fear of witnessing to others (not just Muslims). First, gaining Cultural Intelligence about Muslim countries is a good place to start. It is possible to educate yourself and take a course on Islam for Christians that will explain in detail all the things covered in this book. Second, pray for the LORD to bring Muslims in your path. I know a bright young woman who did not know a single Muslim person but had the desire to share the Gospel with them. As she began to pray, she began to not only see more Muslims in her path, but they began to open the conversation! She met her first Muslim friend at the library. They ended up in a conversation that developed into a friendship and mutual respect for one another. The woman even invited her to her University's Muslim Student Association event as her honored guest, where she met a large number of Muslims who attend her college! What a praise!

What does it mean to Share the Gospel?

I did not learn how to do evangelism. In the beginning of my Christian life, I was told by well-meaning people that sharing my testimony was the same thing as sharing the Gospel. Your testimony can be a powerful, personal way to make a connection with another, but it is NOT the Gospel.

I was recently told by a Christian woman that she shared the Gospel with a Muslim woman who had been suffering from depression. I praised God and asked her what she said to the woman. She told me that she told the young woman that God loves her. When I pressed her a bit more about the specific things she conveyed to the woman, she said that she told her that Jesus loves her and that God loves all He has created. While that is a very kind thing to do, it is not the Gospel. John 3:16 does start with "For God so loved the world..." but it does not end there. The rest of the verse tells us that He sent His one and only begotten (KJV) Son and those who do not believe are under God's judgment and stand condemned. *"For God so loved the world, that he gave his only Son, that whoever believes in him should not perish but have eternal life. For God did not send his Son into the world to condemn the world, but in order that the world might be saved through him. Whoever believes in him is not condemned, but whoever does not believe is condemned already, because he has not believed in the name of the only Son of God (John 3:16-18)."* Therefore, we also need to share explicitly the reason why Jesus came, His life, His death and resurrection in order to connect the dots to God and Christ.

As a Muslim, people told me that God loves me (to which I would sarcastically answer "so what?," and that made people stop talking to me) and others told me "Jesus loves you" (which someone shouted at me from a passing car - still not sure what to make of that). Muslims believe that there are 99 most holy names of Allah -- ***none of those are "love."*** Love is not a part of the bargain Allah strikes with Muslims on Judgment Day. None of these people explained who Jesus was or if the belief was anything different than what I already known about Isa Masih.

A few years later, I was asked to speak about evangelism at a gathering and asked to share how I defend Christianity to Muslims. While we need to know what are the key differences between Islam and Christianity in order to make a defense for our faith, apologetics is not evangelism either. At other times, I have seen those who wish to get into arguments with Muslims about how Jesus is the Son of God (not realizing that Muslims consider that to be blasphemous or have a totally different definition of "son" as in a physical son) and it has been downright embarrassing to watch the exchange. Arguments can leave both sides frustrated and angry. None of these are ways to evangelize.

The Gospel is the story of how human beings try to work their way to God on their own merit and don't succeed because we are sinful from birth (Psalm 51). It is the resplendent testimony of Jesus Christ Himself who came down and dwelt among us. Did you know that Christianity is the **ONLY** religion where God Himself comes down to His people? All other religions put the burden on the individual, except in Christianity. This sets Jesus apart from all others.

There is a magnificent verse in the book of Isaiah that says "For thus says the One who is high and lifted up, who inhabits eternity, whose name is Holy: "I dwell in the high and holy place, and also with him who is of a contrite and lowly spirit, to revive the spirit of the lowly, and to revive the heart of the contrite (Isaiah 57:15)." The Lord is near to the brokenhearted and through Christ, He saw it fit to come down and to tend to His sheep Himself. This is the very heart of God.

Jesus Christ is the only sinless person to ever exist. He was fully God and fully human. He was crucified on the cross for the remission of our sins and paid the penalty for sin by pouring out His blood - the same blood that covers us. He was the perfect sacrifice that God accepted. He was buried in a sealed tomb and after three days, He rose again from the dead, claiming victory over death. He ascended into heaven and sits on the right hand of God the Father Almighty and He will come back on Judgment Day to judge the quick and the dead. This is the Gospel of the Good News we are called to share. The most succinct presentation of the Gospel I have found is in the Apostle's Creed, which was written in the second or third century.[30]

Bridge the GOSPEL

But you will receive power when the Holy Spirit has come upon you, and you will be my witnesses in Jerusalem and in all Judea and Samaria, and to the end of the earth."
Acts 1:8

It is difficult to explain God's love to a Muslim person. There is no personal relationship with Allah. He is far removed from earth in life and even in death. He does not even participate in Paradise and truly wants nothing to do with humans. The relationship of the Trinity makes no sense for the Muslim person and neither does the relationship of the body of Christ or of us as adopted children of God. Just as the previous chapters had terms about Islam from Arabic, these were foreign terms to me, even as an English speaker and were equally as puzzling to me as a new believer.

---

[30] What is the Apostle's Creed? Billy Graham Evangelistic Association (2004). https://billygraham.org/answer/what-is-the-apostles-creed/

Bridge the GOSPEL

And how can they preach unless they are sent? As it is written: "How beautiful are the feet of those who bring good news!" ~ Romans 10:15

1 Step

2 Steps

3 Steps

4 Steps

No GRACE	No LOVE	No TRUE WITNESS	No RELATIONSHIPS
It's what you DO in ISLAM & in EVERY OTHER RELIGION!	99 Names for ALLAH– not a single one is "LOVE"	Good to be the hands & feet of Christ, but need to SAY the WORDS!	NOT a PROJECT – it's a Human Being with an eternal SOUL. Jesus formed Relationships!

Mona Sabah Earnest 2018

Jesus invited His people into the mission of God: to bring all nations to Him. This is not a little invitation. I believe that in seeing Jesus as our Messiah, we forget sometimes that He is also the King of the Universe.

I have a passion for reading historical biographies. I have read several about the ancient European Kings and Queens and I am keenly fascinated by Tudor England. I think it's the amount of power they wielded during the time of exploration of the New World during the 1400's. In the old days, the King of a nation would send out a chosen representative. He would provide them with papers bearing his seal and trust them with the power of the signet ring which would be taken off his hand. The signet ring (note the root word "sign") had the seal of the Kingdom imprinted upon it. One who had the signet ring had signature authority of the Sovereign. This was a vast amount of power and representation of their nation. It also showed a great deal of certainty and reliance on the King's part. We as Christ followers are given His seal-- the Holy Spirit. We are bearers of His signature around the world and serve as the representatives of the Kingdom of God to others. What an honor!

Imagine getting a personal invitation from someone you hold in high esteem. All our earthly examples fall short here, but just to draw a comparison, think about the CEO of a major corporation. Imagine this person wrote you a letter and asked you to join them in an endeavor. Wouldn't that be something to tell your friends and family about? How exciting to be chosen to do something alongside such a great person!

The closest I ever came to this brush with fame was when I used to work for the Campbell Soup Company. The billionaire grandson of the founder John Dorrance was going to personally visit the manufacturing plant in Sacramento, California where I worked in Human Resources. Out of all the 1400 employees, I was chosen to be one of a handful who got to shake hands with him. We spent weeks in a frenzied preparation and high anticipation of this noteworthy visit. We were also to join him on a project he was doing for the organization. Everyone was in a flurry of activity and we even had to tell our Vice President what we were going to wear on that auspicious day.

We behave this way for a human, yet we fall short of preparation, anticipation or even in our feeble attempt to do something for the maker of Heaven and Earth. We are called more than just an ancillary presence, we are called "ambassadors of Christ." "Therefore, we are ambassadors for

Christ, God making his appeal through us. We implore you on behalf of Christ, be reconciled to God (2 Corinthians 5:20)."

My question to you is: Do you behave like an ambassador for Jesus Christ? An ambassador is defined by the Merriam-Webster dictionary as "an official envoy; *especially* : a diplomatic agent of the highest rank accredited to a foreign government or sovereign as the resident representative of his or her own government or sovereign or appointed for a special and often temporary diplomatic assignment" or another definition is "an authorized representative or messenger."[31] We are not only an envoy of the Sovereign King, but also a bearer of His life-giving, life-changing Gospel of Good News to a world that only has bad news.

The Lord is working in such a mighty way today through all nations. There are more Muslims who have accepted Jesus Christ as their Lord and Savior in this century than all other centuries combined. Here are some sources for these statistics:

a. Indonesia: church grown to over 20 million
  http://www.leaderu.com/theology/islaminamerica.html
b. Iran: 1979, estimate was 500 Christians. 2014 estimates: 370,000, in 2015 that number increased to 450,000 and growing.
  https://opentheword.org/2017/09/01/muslim-cleric-warns-of-explosive-growth-of-christianity-among-iranian-youth/
c. China: From 1 million (Communist takeover in 1949) to over 100 million followers, in 60 years and is being compared to the growth of Christianity in the 4th century!

---

[31] "Ambassador." *Merriam-Webster.com*. Merriam-Webster, n.d. Web. 9 June 2018. https://www.merriam-webster.com/dictionary/ambassador.

Fenngang, Yang (2018). Christianity's Growth in China. https://berkleycenter.georgetown.edu/responses/christianity-s-growth-in-china-and-its-contributions-to-freedoms

Persecution is to be expected according to the Bible. This not only includes persecution for those who wish to share the Gospel (especially in over 50 countries where it is illegal to even bring a Bible into the country), but also a greater punishment sometimes for those who convert to Christianity. Yet, the New Testament bears testimony to many martyrs who gladly gave their life for the Gospel of Christ. Persecution strengthens the church and causes believers to scatter to other places, bringing the light of Christ wherever they go. Many have compared the scattered believers to the embers of fire, or to starfish, which when cut, can regenerate into new starfish. God has given us physical truths for spiritual ones so we may see His design in all nature. Tertullian[32], an early church leader around 185 AD correctly wrote "The blood of the martyrs is the seed of the church."

As the Church, we need to be in prayer for the persecuted Christians around the world. If we are to be the body of Christ (1 Corinthians 12:12-14), we should indeed feel the pain of those who are suffering for their faith and offer help or support. There are several respectable organizations that help underground missionaries do the work of the kingdom. We should also rejoice that through this suffering and perseverance, the Lord brings a rich harvest of converts.

Be Prepared

In order to share the Gospel, one should follow the path of the disciples in the book of Acts. They first prayed together and

---

[32] "Tertullian." GotQuestions.org. https://www.gotquestions.org/Tertullian.html

asked for the Holy Spirit to guide them. The testimony that the Lord gave you concerning His Son is a wonderful starting point for any conversation. There is a good way to share your testimony by identifying what your life was like before Christ (I call this "B.C."), what it is like today with Jesus, and how you see His Holy Spirit working in you to bring you peace, joy, and other fruit of the Spirit from Galatians 5 (I call this "A.D" for after death - after your spiritual death and being made alive in Christ again). When you can identify this in a sentence or two, it becomes easier to share the Gospel in a succinct manner.

People get anxious about not only sharing their testimony, but also talking about Jesus. The beauty of talking to Muslims is that they don't mind talking about spiritual matters. In fact, many of my Western friends are amazed that Muslims get animated and want to talk about God. My way of approaching the topic is to simply ask my Muslim friends and family "What do you know about Jesus?" Invite them to share what they know and how they feel about Him. The answers might just surprise you! While they are speaking, pray that the Holy Spirit gives you the right words to share. Once they have opened the conversation to you, the conversation will allow you to see the gaps in knowledge or maybe they will even ask you a question about a prophet. The key here is to always talk about the One we owe our Salvation to-- Jesus Christ.

There are a few places where we can help to make the connection back to Christ:
His miraculous birth (Matthew 1:18-23, prophesied in Isaiah 7:14), Giver of Life (John 5:21), Healer (Matthew 12:22, Mark 1:34), Forgiver of sins (Luke 5:20), conquered death (Matt 28:6), Just Judge (John 5:22-24). The last one is extremely important because of the Muslim belief of Judgment Day: almost all Sunni

Muslims believe it will be Jesus Christ who comes back to judge all mankind for their good and bad deeds.

Be Obedient

Another reason for sharing the Gospel is because Jesus told all believers to do so in the Great Commission in Matthew 28: 18-20 *"And Jesus came up and spoke to them, saying, "All authority has been given to Me in heaven and on earth. "Go therefore and make disciples of all the nations, baptizing them in the name of the Father and the Son and the Holy Spirit, teaching them to observe all that I commanded you; and lo, I am with you always, even to the end of the age."*
The sad truth is that we are not being obedient and we are not "going." According to most Christian missionary sites, there is only 1 dedicated missionary for every 420,000 Muslims (over 1.8 billion Muslims globally)[33]. There are many Muslims who are genuinely seeking God - I know, for I was one of them!

Romans 10:17 states "So faith comes from hearing, and hearing from the word of Christ." Not only do we need to get off our couch and out of our comfortable cocoons, we need to pray fervently that the Lord brings Muslims and other non-believers into our lives. Since we will not "go," I believe that the Lord is bringing them here -- in droves! What a praise! We can freely share the Gospel in a country that gives us not only the freedom of speech, but also the freedom to worship.

Muslims do not have assurance of Salvation. There is no guarantee that Paradise will be given to them even if they do all the things they are commanded to do. Can you imagine not

---

[33] The Mission. i2 Ministries. June 9, 2018. https://i2ministries.org/the-mission/

knowing if you have been forgiven until after you die? Muslims live with this fear daily. Those who are devout seek to please God and do His will. They try to be obedient, but always fall short of the glory of God -- and that's exactly what Romans 3:19-25 states:

> " Now we know that whatever the law says it speaks to those who are under the law, so that every mouth may be stopped, and the whole world may be held accountable to God. For by works of the law no human being will be justified in his sight, since through the law comes knowledge of sin.
>
> But now the righteousness of God has been manifested apart from the law, although the Law and the Prophets bear witness to it — the righteousness of God through faith in Jesus Christ for all who believe. For there is no distinction: for all have sinned and fall short of the glory of God, and are justified by his grace as a gift, through the redemption that is in Christ Jesus, whom God put forward as a propitiation by his blood, to be received by faith. This was to show God's righteousness, because in his divine forbearance he had passed over former sins."

Sharing the Gospel means stepping outside your comfort zone and see others the way Jesus sees them. He will give you the time, the opportunity, the desire, and the words - you only have to ask God!

Practical Ways to Connect with Muslims

1. PRAY

Prayer is the most powerful weapon we have against the spiritual forces. Prayer opens up the power of heaven and allows us to plug into the Holy Spirit's prompting. Do not depend on yourself to have the smooth speech. Ask God's Holy Spirit to share words that give life to others and are wrapped in love. Pray that the Lord will lift the physical and spiritual veil for Muslims. I like to pray " But when one turns to the Lord, the veil is removed. Now the Lord is the Spirit, and where the Spirit of the Lord is, there is freedom. And we all, with unveiled face, beholding the glory of the Lord are being transformed into the same image from one degree of glory to another. For this comes from the Lord who is the Spirit (2 Corinthians 3:16-18)."

2. MAKE EYE CONTACT

This is a bit difficult to do especially if a woman is wearing a full burqa or a hijab/niqab, but still try to do it. A genuine smile is the start of any authentic relationship! Sometimes, we get into a hurry and don't listen to what God is telling us. A quick prayer and a cheerful greeting may bring about a beautiful friendship with someone from a diverse background.

3. EXTEND HOSPITALITY

Why do we have beautiful homes and we never invite anyone in? Why do we have nice kitchens and never offer to cook for anyone? Hospitality is a part of the culture for Muslims. It used to be this way for Americans as well as well as the early church in Acts 2! The first Christians met together in' homes, worshiped and broke bread together.

In our busy lifestyles, no one has time to cook or even set out a bowl of fruit. Extend an invitation – it doesn't have to be a four-course meal. A genuine desire to make a connection and a simple cup of coffee or tea will do!

4. TALK ABOUT JESUS!

Jesus Christ is who I want to talk about all the time anyway, so why not ask what they think of Him... you might be surprised! If that's too risky for you, ask how your new Muslim friend sees God. Ask them to define His character and see where that conversation goes. Muslims can be very pious. Most enjoy talking about God!

5. SHARE THE GOOD NEWS

Many Christians leave out the most important part. I have heard people say "Well, I want to show Christ in my actions." That is wonderful and what we should do daily to show the love of Christ through our hands and feet. However, that's not the beginning of the story. How will they know if they never hear who Christ is and of His sacrifice for us on the cross? How will they know that God gave us salvation and His grace as a free gift? We cannot earn our way to heaven. ONLY CHRIST has paid our debt, bridged the gap to God and will come back to judge all.

6. BE PATIENT!

This is a relationship... not a pet project. A Muslim is a real person - a human being with feelings and emotions. They are a person connected to a family and a community. They need love and respect and deserve to be treated with kindness. On average, it takes a Muslim about 7 years to accept Christ (however, the Holy Spirit can move at any time, as in my case!). Remember, there is a lot at stake, with family, inheritance, culture and it's usually not an overnight decision. After conversion, be ready to be their family, to disciple your friend & don't leave them to wither on the vine.

Evangelism encompasses a deeper matter of sharing your love, compassion and care for a hurting world. These are ways you can reach anyone (not just Muslims). If your heart is in the right place and you have prepared yourself with the word of the Lord, God will help you! You are not on your own.

I have the "Practical Steps" information on a free, easy to reference bookmark on my blog post titled "Reaching Muslims in Love[34]" that you can print out for your own use.

---

[34] https://monaearnest.wordpress.com/2017/05/11/reaching-muslims-in-love/

1. _____ & _____ cannot exist together for a
   Christian.

2. We need to speak the words of the Gospel.

3. We need to _____ our enemies and _____
   for those who persecute you (Matthew 5:44).

4. More Muslims are coming to Christ in this century than all
centuries combined.   TRUE or FALSE

5. Scattered believers who are persecuted can also be compared
to _____ or _____ because of the multiplying
effect they have.

APPLICATION

What are 3 things you learned about Evangelism to Muslims in this Chapter?

_____

_____

_____

Is there someone you need to pray for on a daily basis?

_____

Is there someone you know who needs to hear the fact that Jesus forgives sins and gives eternal life to those who believe in Him as Lord and Savior?

_____

How will you teach your family or friends this information?

_____

_____

Chapter 7

Muslim Objections to Christ

For the word of the cross is folly to those who are perishing, but to us who are being saved it is the power of God.

1 Corinthians 1:18

As mentioned in the previous chapters, there are two main objections to Christianity: Jesus as the son of God and also the claim that the Bible is corrupt. This chapter will address issues that seem to crop up in almost every conversation I have ever had with a Muslim person. These are also the exact same objections I had when I was a Muslim. In fact, my mind was closed off to both issues, as I had resolved early on in my life that they were both the truth and firmly established as fact in the Quran. **I liked what I heard about the God Christians worshiped (who I thought was the same as Allah) but I did not want anything to do with the "Son."**

In my first book, I shared my testimony about when I first heard about the Trinity. The pastor teaching the class we were attending said that Jesus was God. This claim was more than I could bear! I wanted to physically cover my ears to the blasphemy I heard and run out of the room. Even though I had asked my husband to go to the class with me, I told him I would never go back if the church taught things like that! Your Muslim friend may have the same reaction to the message you bring.

There are differences in understanding of the terms used in English and also in Christianity. This discrepancy can quickly cause a communication breakdown.

First Objection: Son of God

"It is not [befitting] for Allah to take a son; exalted is He! When He decrees an affair, He only says to it, 'Be,' and it is (Surah 19:35)."

Jesus Christ is accepted only as a prophet of Allah and as a man. Nothing else. The first belief for Muslims is a **daily** prayer that includes the denial of the deity of Christ. The trinity is not only seen as blasphemous polytheistic worship of God, Jesus and Mary, but also implies a sexual encounter of Allah with Mary, resulting in Jesus as a half-man, half-god. When explaining to Christians, I use the example of the Greek god Zeus coming down and having a physical encounter with a female mortal and thus producing a demi-god.

Of course, when stated this way, one can better understand why the claim is so offensive to the notion of worshiping one God. This is another reason they vehemently deny the triune God - God in three persons and the Trinity of God the Father, Christ the Son and the Holy Spirit. Jesus' virgin birth is affirmed by the Quran (as well as the Bible), along with the statement of Mary's purity at the time of conception through a divine miracle.

When Jesus taught His disciples to pray in Matthew 6:9-13, he taught them to say "Our Father..." I have had family members who bristle at this because they say "God is not

your Father, nor the father to anyone else including Jesus."
Muslims see Allah as the master and themselves as slaves.
As mentioned in the previous chapter, the father and son
relationship for God implies a physical, sexual procreation
with Mary. It is the height of blasphemy for Muslims... and
for Christians! Muslims are surprised when they tell me that
they are offended by Christians who tell them that Jesus is
the son of God. The next step in the conversation would be
to ask the Muslim person what they mean by "the son of
God." Some Muslims will get uncomfortable at this question
while others will be blunt about the physical relationship
with Mary.

According to the Qur'an, "It is not befitting to (the majesty
of) Allah that He should beget a son" (Surah Maryam 19:35).
Surah al-Ikhlas ("The Sincerity") is a chapter that all Muslims
are instructed to memorize. So great is the reward for this
special prayer that confirms the Tawhid (oneness of Allah)
that Muslims are told that if they recite it three times, it is the
same as reading the entire Quran. They will also get a
special "credit" (sawaab - good works) for doing this. These
verses are also said regularly during prayer five times a day
in the life of a devout Muslim.

There is a Hadith that verifies this:
Abu Sa`id said: The Messenger of Allah said to his
Companions, "Is any of you incapable of reciting one third
of the Qur'an in a night?" They felt burdened by this, and so
they asked, "Which of us has the capability for that, O
Messenger of Allah?!" He said, "[Allah has divided the
Qur'an into three parts, and Qul-HuwAllahu-Ahad], is one-
third of the Qur'an." (Bukhari 6643).[35]

I memorized this Surah at a young age and it was near and dear to me. It brought me great joy to gain extra credit works whenever I recited it. These verses represent the essence of Islam and carry great weight because of what Muhammad said about them.

The Surah and prayer says the following:

بِسْمِ اللَّهِ الرَّحْمَٰنِ الرَّحِيمِ
In the name of Allah, the Beneficent, the Merciful.
قُلْ هُوَ اللَّهُ أَحَدٌ
Say: He, Allah, is One. (112:1)
اللَّهُ الصَّمَدُ
Allah is He on Whom all depend (112:2)
لَمْ يَلِدْ وَلَمْ يُولَدْ
He begets not, nor is He begotten. (112:3)
وَلَمْ يَكُنْ لَهُ كُفُوًا أَحَدٌ
And none is like Him. (112:4)

In the Bible, the term "begotten" in reference to the Father and the Son does NOT signify sexual reproduction but explicitly refers to a special, supernatural relationship. In one of the most widely recognized verses in the Bible, John 3:16, it states " For God so loved the world, that he gave his only begotten Son, that whoever believes in him should not perish but have eternal life. (KJV)" The apostle John was not implying anything physical, but was pointing out the unique divine nature of Christ. John also states, " No one has ever seen God; the only God, who is at the Father's side, he has made him known" (John 1:18). While Christians are the

---

[35] "Meaning of Hadith Qul Huwaa Allahu Ahad" (2008).
https://islamqa.info/en/10022

children of God through adoption in Christ, Jesus is God (second person of the Trinity) and is co-equal and co-eternal. *Shirk* is considered the ultimate blasphemy and sin in Islam. Shirk means to ascribe partners to Allah and make them equal to him.

The Quran says "Indeed, Allah does not forgive association with Him, but He forgives what is less than that for whom He wills. And he who associates others with Allah has certainly gone far astray (Surah an Nisa 4:116)." In Islam, Jesus is merely the only sinless human to ever exist and a prophet. He has been given great power through the miracles of healing the sick, exorcising demons, and power to raise dead to life (more than any other prophet including Muhammad) but they deny His deity or that He came as God in human flesh. Even though there is extra-Biblical, historic evidence to the crucifixion of Christ, the Qur'an denies it and instead affirms, "they killed him not, nor crucified him, but so it was made to appear to them (Surah an Nisa 4:157)."

To help connect the dots from previous chapters, Surah al Ikhlas is similar to the prayer recited in the ear of the newborn. The daily call to prayer (broadcasted from the minarets in the mosque) is called the adhan (or azan). Anyone who visits or lives in a Muslim country will hear the call to prayer five times a day - you automatically memorize it early on in life. Again, it broadcasts the news that there is **no one but Allah**. The adhan[36] is as follows:

---

[36] https://www.alislam.org/library/book/salat/adhan-or-the-muslim-call-to-prayer/

ADHAN

اَللهُ اَكْبَرُ

Transliteration: Allahu Akbar (four times)
Translation: *Allah is the Greatest* (Recited four times)

اَشْهَدُ اَن لَا اِلهَ الاَ اللهُ

Transliteration: Ash-hadu alla ilaha illallah (twice)
Translation: *I bear witness that there is none worthy of worship except Allah* (Recited twice)

اَشْهَدُ اَنَّ مُحَمَّدًا رَسُولُ اللهِ

Transliteration: Ash-hadu anna Muhammadar Rasulullah (twice)
Translation: *I bear witness that Muhammad is the Messenger of Allah.* (Recited twice)

حَيٌّ عَلَى الصَّلوةِ

Transliteration: Hayya alassalah (twice)
Translation: *Come to Prayer* (Recited twice)

حَيٌّ عَلَى الفَلاَحِ

Transliteration: Hayya alal-Falah (twice)
Translation: *Come to success.* (Recited twice)

اَللهُ اَكْبَرُ.

Transliteration: Allahu Akbar (twice)
Translation:*Allah is the Greatest.* (Recited twice)

لَا اِلهَ اِلاَ اللهُ

Transliteration: La ilaha illallah
Translation: *There is none worthy of worship except Allah.*

"We like your God, but not the SON"

The Response

"For God so loved the world, that he gave his only begotten Son, that whoever believes in him should not perish but have eternal life (John 3:16)."
To reject God's gift of his Son is to reject God Himself.

"Whoever listens to you listens to me; whoever rejects you rejects me; but whoever rejects me rejects him who sent me (Luke 10:16)."

Quran
<u>Taurat (Torah referenced 18 times):</u> "He hath revealed unto thee (Muhammad) the Scripture with truth, confirming that which was (revealed) before it, even as He revealed the Torah and the Gospel (Surah 3:3)."
<u>Zabur (Psalms referenced 3 times):</u> Surah an Nisa 4:163 of the Qur'an states "and to David We gave the Psalms." Therefore, Islam claims the Psalms as being inspired of God.
<u>Injeel (Gospel referenced 12 times):</u> "Injil" is Arabic for "euaggelion" in Greek= evangel. Usually combined with Taurat in Quran.

Quran
"We sent after them Jesus son of Mary, and bestowed on him the Gospel; and **We ordained in the hearts of those who followed him Compassion and Mercy** (Surah 57:27)."
The Quranic expression "Bismillah al-Rahman al-Rahim" said at the start of everything credits this to Allah: "In the name of Allah, most **gracious, most merciful.**"

Seems to indicate that Christians are bestowed with the character of God!

135

Jesus' Response

"The Father judges no one, but has entrusted all judgment to the Son, that all may honor the Son just as they honor the Father. Whoever does not honor the Son does not honor the Father, who sent him (John 5:22–23)."

"It is written in the Prophets, 'And they will all be taught by God.' Everyone who has heard and learned from the Father comes to me (John 6:45)."

"I am the way and the truth and the life. No one comes to the Father except through me (John 14:6)."

Our Response

"Salvation is found in no one else, for there is no other name under heaven given to mankind by which we must be saved (Acts 4:12)."

"For there is one God, and there is one mediator between God and mankind, the man Christ Jesus (1 Tim. 2:5)."

"No one who denies the Son has the Father; whoever acknowledges the Son has the Father also (1 John 2:23)."

Second Objection: Bible is CORRUPT

There are numerous passages in the Quran that attest to the truths that have been given down to Moses (Taurat-Torah), David (Zabur - Psalms), and Jesus (Injeel - New Testament Gospel). Then, the Quran seems to take a downturn and say that all have been twisted. It is important to note that the Quran calls Jews and Christians "People of the Book," for they recognize God as the one who gave out his word through these men as important prophets.

"Can ye (o ye men of Faith) entertain the hope that they will believe in you?- Seeing that a party of them heard the Word of Allah, and perverted it knowingly after they understood it... Then woe to those who write the Book with their own hands, and then say:"This is from Allah," to traffic with it for miserable price!- Woe to them for what their hands do write, and for the gain they make thereby (Surah al Baqarah 2:75,79)."

"Indeed, those who conceal what We sent down of clear proofs and guidance after We made it clear for the people in the Scripture - those are cursed by Allah and cursed by those who curse (Surah al Baqarah 2:159)."

"Indeed, they who conceal what Allah has sent down of the Book and exchange it for a small price - those consume not into their bellies except the Fire. And Allah will not speak to them on the Day of Resurrection, nor will He purify them. And they will have a painful punishment (Surah al Baqarah 2:174)."

"There is among them a section who distort the Book with their tongues: (As they read) you would think it is a part of the Book, but it is no part of the Book; and they say, "That is from Allah," but it is not from Allah: It is they who tell a lie against Allah, and (well) they know it! (Surah Ali 'Imran 3:78)."

"And [mention, O Muhammad], when Allah took a covenant from those who were given the Scripture, [saying], "You must make it clear to the people and not conceal it." But they threw it away behind their backs and exchanged it for a small price. And wretched is that which they purchased (Surah Ali 'Imran 3:187)."

"Among the Jews are those who distort words from their [proper] usages and say, "We hear and disobey" and "Hear but be not heard" and "Ra'ina," twisting their tongues and defaming the religion. And if they had said [instead], "We hear and obey" and "Wait for us [to understand]," it would have been better for them and more suitable. But Allah has cursed them for their disbelief, so they believe not, except for a few (Surah an Nisa 4:46)."

"But because of their breach of their covenant, We cursed them, and made their hearts grow hard; they change the words from their (right) places and forget a good part of the message that was sent them, nor wilt thou cease to find them- barring a few - ever bent on (new) deceits: but forgive them, and overlook (their misdeeds): for Allah loveth those who are kind. From those, too, who call themselves Christians, We did take a covenant, but they forgot a good part of the message that was sent them: so we estranged them, with enmity and hatred between the one and the other, to the day of judgment. And soon will Allah show them what it is they have done (Surah al Ma'idah 5:13-14)."

"O People of the Scripture, there has come to you Our Messenger making clear to you much of what you used to conceal of the Scripture and overlooking much. There has come to you from Allah a light and a clear Book (Surah al Ma'idah 5:15)."

"No just estimate of Allah do they make when they say: "Nothing doth Allah send down to man (by way of revelation)" Say: "Who then sent down the Book which Moses brought?- a light and guidance to man: But ye make it into (separate) sheets for show, while ye conceal much (of its contents): therein were ye taught that which ye knew not-neither ye nor your fathers." Say: "Allah (sent it down)": Then leave them to plunge in vain discourse and trifling (Surah al An'am 6:91)."

"But those who wronged among them changed [the words] to a statement other than that which had been said to them. So We sent upon them a punishment from the sky for the wrong that they were doing (Surah al A'raf 7:162)."

Hadith

The people of the Book used to read the Torah in Hebrew and then explain it in Arabic to the Muslims. Allah's Apostle said (to the Muslims). "Do not believe the people of the Book, nor disbelieve them, but say, 'We believe in Allah and whatever is revealed to us, and whatever is revealed to you '"(Bukhari 92, 460).

Quran SUPPORT

Sura 5:47, which states, "Let the people of the gospel judge by what God has sent down therein. Whosoever judges not by that which God has sent down—it is they who are iniquitous."
This Quran verse assumes the reliability of the gospel (thus Christian Scripture) & expects Christians to live by it.
Sura 3:55 Allah speaks to Jesus, saying, "[W]hen he said, "O Jesus, I shall take thee and raise thee unto me, and purify thee of those who disbelieved, and place those who followed thee above those who disbelieved, until the day of resurrection. Then unto me is your return, and I shall judge between you concerning that wherein you used to differ."

If corrupted, then why does the Quran quote the Bible?

A Hadith of great importance shows that Muhammad drew from at least one of the Apostle Paul's writings:
Abu Huraira told that after God's messenger had stated that God most high has said, "I have prepared for my upright servants what eye has not seen, nor ear heard, nor has entered into the heart of man," he added, "Recite, if you wish, 'No soul knows what comfort has been concealed for them'." (Bukhari and Muslim). If one looks at 1 Corinthians 2:9, "But as it is written, Eye hath not seen, nor ear heard, neither have entered into the heart of man, the things which God hath prepared for them that love him." The Bible of course came hundreds of years before the Quran. The verse from 1 Corinthians is almost taken verbatim. So, the question becomes a bit more weighty - why would Allah use a verse from the Bible if it was not to be trusted?

Evidence for the Bible

It may help to see the chronology of when the Bible came together versus the dates for the Quran. When I speak about Islam, I find that many are confused about when Muhammad lived and some would even go as far as to date him to around the same time as Christ. The truth is that Islam came upon the scene six hundred years later!

__Codex Sinaiticus__ (c. 350) contains the oldest complete copy of the New Testament, as well as most of the Greek Old Testament, known as the *Septuagint.*
__Codex Vaticanus Graecus__ 1209 (c. 300-325) is one of the best available Greek manuscripts of almost the entire bible.
__Codex Alexandrinus__ (c. 400-440) Complete Bible

Chronology		
BIBLE	**QURAN**	
33 AD — Jesus Death	570-632 AD — Muhammad	
48-64 — Paul's Letters	765 — Sira (Ibn Ishaq)	
50-66 — Gospels : Matthew, Mark, & Luke	833 — Sira Ibn Hisham	
52-62 — Acts	870 — Hadith Bukhari	
92 — John	923 — Hadith Tabari	
393 AD — Bible Old Testament and New Testament (27 books) Canonized by Council of Hippo	1924 — Quran Canonized in Cairo for first time	
265 Complete Manuscripts Found - 27 Books Over 6000 New Testament	**6 Manuscripts Found – None complete**	

There are thousands of ways to compare the validity of the Bible to the Quran. However, this information is presented to the reader as education and not to provide ammunition for an argument. Muslims are very sensitive about anything they perceive to be an insult hurled towards their book. The goal is to open the dialogue - not to close it. It is important, however for Christians to understand how many brilliant minds have tested and tried the word of God as revealed in the Bible. All come away with a stronger validity of the proof of claim. The bottom line is that that even the reader here does not have to believe me. You can see for yourself by doing your own research.

Questions to Ask

WHEN and **WHERE** was the Bible corrupted since the Quran says that the Torah, the Psalms, and the Gospel are from Allah and Allah's words cannot be changed?"
Why would Muhammad tell Muslims in the Quran to believe in three books (Torah, Psalms, and Gospel) that were corrupted?

Mark 13:31 - Heaven and earth will pass away, but My words will never pass away.
Matthew 5:18 - For I tell you truly, until heaven and earth pass away, not a single jot, not a stroke of a pen, will disappear from the Law until everything is accomplished.

If God is sovereign, then why can His word be changed by man?

How to Respectfully Engage in a Dialogue?

Pray... earnestly PRAY:
For the LORD to change your own heart and see Muslims with His eyes.
For the LORD to bring the unsaved to you!
For the LORD to give you the words that speak life.

Understand that Muslims are not Islam.
Many have little or no understanding of the Quran.
Many do not speak Arabic as their native tongue.
Many are trying to be devout in order to earn God's favor!

"God shows his love for us in that while we were still sinners, Christ died for us"

Romans 5:8

*"While we were **enemies** we were reconciled to God by the death of his Son, much more, now that we are reconciled, shall we be saved by his life"*

Romans 5:10

As Christians, we should remember that there was a time when we were in almost the same place - we thought that we could live our life the way we wanted, according to our own rules and desires. There is a great multitude of souls who do not yet know Christ as Lord and Savior. They believe in their own god and that their own works or merit will bring them great pleasure. The things of this world leave us hollow and wanting more. They are like cotton candy -- sweet in the mouth but ephemeral as it wastes away into nothing. May the Lord give each Christian a hunger and an urgency to share the Gospel of Good News to a world that is perishing. Millions die without ever having heard of what Jesus Christ has done on the cross for the remission of sins. This should be our one desire - to see the Lord glorified and lifted up as every tongue, tribe and nation bows their knees and believes that Jesus Christ is King.

APPLICATION

What are ways you will address-

Jesus as the Son of God:
_____

Bible as the Inerrant Word of God:
_____

How will you share the Gospel with those who are lost?
_____

How will you use the information presented in this book?

_____
_____
_____
_____

The Rest of Mona's Testimony

There is work to be done for God's Kingdom and many people from other countries can be found right here in the United States. I moved to America when I was ten years old and when I was 35, the Good News was finally shared with me. The impact was so great that I accepted Christ as Lord immediately when the words of the Gospel fell upon my ears! What a shame that I did not have an authentic witness in my life who shared the pure Gospel with me for 25 years while I lived here in the United States. I cannot help but think about my paternal and maternal grandparents who died before they heard the Gospel. The most heart-wrenching part for me to think about is my beloved nanny, Abbai, who died without knowing Jesus Christ as her Lord.

May this book be a call to action for the sleeping Church. How many more Muslims will pass away without hearing the Gospel? There should be a sense of urgency in our own life to share the Gospel with a world that has no hope. I have a deep love for my Muslim family and friends. Sharing the Gospel is the best way to show each one how much they are loved, not only by us but truly loved by the One who gave up His life and paid the penalty of sin on the cross - Christ Jesus.

For from the rising of the sun to its setting my name will be great among the nations, and in every place incense will be offered to my name, and a pure offering. For my name will be great among the nations, says the LORD of hosts.

Malachi 1:11

About the Author

Mona Sabah Earnest was born and raised in the Middle East (Saudi Arabia, Kuwait and United Arab Emirates), England, went to school in Pakistan and then finally moved to the United States. She speaks English, Spanish, and Urdu fluently. She has worked in the Human Resources field and teaches Management, Leadership and Cultural Diversity. She holds her Masters in Human Resources from the University of San Francisco. She is a professional speaker and a corporate trainer.

Mona became a follower of Jesus Christ at the age of 35. She has been married to her husband Stephen since 1993 and has three beautiful children. Her mission statement is: *To be a light for the Kingdom of God by sharing my testimony of faith in my Lord & Savior Jesus Christ and by equipping the Church to be an authentic witness to share the Gospel.*

She published her testimony "From Isa to Christ: A Muslim Woman's Search for the Hand of God" in February 2017. It is available on Amazon, Kindle and wherever books are sold.

This book is also presented as a course and seminar. Please contact her if you are interested in bringing it to your area.

BLOG: https://monaearnest.wordpress.com/

FACEBOOK: Mona Sabah Earnest

AUTHOR PAGE: https://www.amazon.com/Mona-Sabah/e/B06X6B13JB

*Please consider leaving a review for this book on Amazon- it would be greatly appreciated.

Appendix of Terms

Frequently Used Terms with Pronunciation:

Abrogation - means to annul or abolish by authoritative action. The Quran declares four earlier passages as null and void, while giving later revelations authority.

Adhan [Ah-dhaan] - Arabic word for call to prayer - same as "azan"

Allah [Ul-lah]- Arabic name for God, meaning one God

Allahuakbar [Ul-lahu-ak-baar]- Arabic saying "God is great" (called the Takbir)

Apostate - One who renounces a religious belief

Burqa [Boor-kah]- A woman's outer garment that covers her (same as Niqab)

Eid-al-Adha [Eed - al- ud-hah] - Festival of the Sacrifice, celebrated 70 days after the end of Ramadan once a year.

Five Pillars of Faith:

    1. Shahadah: reciting the Muslim profession of faith.
    2. Salat: ritual prayers in the proper way five times daily.
    3. Zakat: paying an alms (or charity) for poor and the needy.

4. Sawm: fasting during the month of Ramadan.

5. Hajj: pilgrimage to Mecca.

Hadith [Haw-deeth]- Traditions of prophet Muhammad

Halal [Ha-lol] - Kosher or Permissible

Hram [Ha-rom] - Unclean or Forbidden

Hijab [Hee-job]- Means to cover (usually face, hair, neck, upper body)

Imam [Ee-mom]- Muslim leader, holy person, or cleric

Injeel [Een-jeel]- Arabic name for the Gospels given by Allah to Isa Masih

Isa [Ee-saw]- Arabic name for Jesus in the Quran, also Isa Masih (Jesus Messiah)

Isa Ibn Maryam - Jesus, son of Mary

Islam [Ee-slaam]- Arabic word for submission or surrender

Jihad [Jee-had] - to struggle or strive with intent - against infidels or to struggle internally

Kaaba [Kaa-bah] - the black cube in Mecca - shrine of worship for Muslims during Hajj

Kafir [Kaw-fir] - Worst name given to an unbeliever and an apostate

Laylat al Qadr - Arabic for night of destiny or night of power

Mahram [Mah-rom] - anyone whom she is permanently forbidden to marry, because of blood ties, breastfeeding or ties through marriage, such as her father, son, or brother

Mehndi [Men-dee]- Ceremony surrounding a paste made from the henna plant

Muhammad or Mohammad (same) - Prophet & founder of Islam. (A.D. 570-A.D. 632)

Mosque [Moss-k]- Place of prayer (also called Masjid [Mass-jed])

Muslim[Moose-slim] - Arabic for "one who submits"

Qibla [Kib-blah] - Arabic for Direction of Prayer towards the Kaaba

Quran [Koor-ahn]- Muslim holy book (also called "Koran"). Arabic word that means "to recite"

Ramadan [Ram-ah-don] - Annual period of 30 days of obligatory fasting for Muslims

Sahih [Saw-heeh] - authentic or valid Hadith

Shia [Shee-ah] - also called "Shiite" by Westerners. The second largest sect of Islam that believes Ali was the successor after Muhammad

Shirk [Shirk] - Ultimate blasphemy of making anyone or anything equal to Allah

Sira [See-rah] - Biography of Muhammad, written in 765 AD

Sunni [Soon-nee] - The major sect of Islam that follows traditions of Muhammad

Surah [Soo-rah] - Arabic word for a Chapter in the Quran

Tawaaf [Tah-wof] - to go around or circumabulate

Taqiyya [Tak-ee-yah] - Sharia states in certain situations, deception – also known as 'taqiyya'(Quran) is not only permitted but obligatory.

Tawhid [Tow-heed] - Arabic word for the Oneness of God. It is the pivotal principle of Islam

Taurat [Tow-raat] - Arabic word for Torah, revealed to Musa (Moses)

Ummah [Uma] - Global community of Muslims

Umrah [Oom-rah] - A lesser or voluntary pilgrimage to Mecca made at anytime

Zabur [Zah-boor] - Arabic word for Psalms, given to Daud (David)

Appendix of Answers

History of Islam

1. Allah is ONE - no more paganism (big practice at that time in Arabia) is stated by the <u>Shahada.</u>
2. Islam means: <u>to submit or surrender to the will of Allah.</u>
3. Quran means: <u>to recite.</u>
4. Hadith are: <u>the teachings or traditions</u> of Muhammad.
5. Sira of Muhammad is a book about the <u>life or biography</u> of Muhammad.
6. Abrogation means <u>annul or abolish by authoritative action.</u>
7. Sahih means <u>authentic or valid.</u>

Muslim Beliefs & Practices

1. Muslims have to pray five times a day and these prayers can be anything they want to say to Allah. TRUE OR **FALSE**
2. Fasting during Ramadan means no food or water between <u>sunrise and sunset.</u>
3. <u>Eid al Adha</u> is the name of the Festival of Sacrifice done <u>70</u> days after the end of Ramadan.
4. The Hajj is the fifth pillar of faith and all Muslims must go to <u>Mecca</u> at least once in their lifetime.

5. Muslims pray in <u>Arabic</u> (language). Whether they speak it or not.
6. Muslims have to do all five pillars as a requirement of their religion. **TRUE** OR FALSE
7. Jihad is one of the 5 Pillars of Islam. TRUE OR **FALSE**
8. Jihad means to <u>struggle or strive with an intent.</u>

Traditions & Convictions

1. Muslims pray before eating, driving, starting anything. **TRUE** or FALSE
2. Jinn are<u>: half human half fire supernatural beings with a body and soul (or also "very scary" could be a correct answer!).</u>
3. The Left Hand is <u>unclean and used for bathroom duties</u> while the Right is <u>clean, used for greeting and eating.</u>
4. Having dogs in a Muslim home means<u> angels </u>will not visit.
5. The physical book of the Quran <u>is the revealed word of Allah.</u>
6. The Muslim will place their Quran on the <u> highest </u> <u>shelf</u> in the house.
7. The Kaaba has a <u> black </u> <u> stone or meteorite </u> that must be kissed during Hajj. It turned from a <u>white</u> color to a <u>black</u> color due to <u>sin.</u>

Women in Islam

1. Women in Islam cannot <u> fast or pray </u> when bleeding.
2. Women in Islam are to be given <u> half </u> the inheritance of a male.
3. <u>Maryam (Mary, mother of Jesus)</u> is the only woman mentioned by name in the entire Quran.

4. Heaven is called <u>Paradise</u> in the Quran and differs from the Bible.
5. Men can have multiple wives on earth and in <u>Paradise.</u>
6. There is no minimum age for girls to marry in Islam.
   TRUE OR FALSE

Understanding Assumptions

TRINITY:
Christians <u> God,   Jesus, &   the Holy Spirit </u>.
Muslims<u> God,   Jesus, &   Mary </u>.

ISLAM:
People think it means <u> peace </u> but it means <u>submission.</u>
One who practices Islam is called a <u>Muslim.</u>
Quran vs. Christ = <u>God's word revealed in a BOOK vs. God's word in Christ </u>.

TEACHINGS
*Allah is <u>ONE</u>. He has no <u> son   or   wife </u>.
*Shirk: <u>ultimate blasphemy to put anyone equivalent to Allah </u>.
*Tawhid means: <u> belief in the oneness of God </u>.
Do Christians and Muslims worship the same God?
TRUE OR **FALSE**

SIN
Quran calls only 1 person sinless or pure and that person is <u>Isa (Jesus) </u>.
Muslims believe their <u> good </u> <u> works </u> can get them to Paradise.
Instead of using the word "sin," we can use the words <u>good</u> deeds & <u>bad </u>deeds.

Evangelism

1. <u>Fear & Faith</u> cannot exist together for a Christian.
2. We need to speak the words of the Gospel.
3. We need to ___<u>love</u>__ our enemies and__<u>pray</u>__ for those who persecute you (Matthew 5:44).
4. More Muslims are coming to Christ in this century than all centuries combined. - **TRUE** or FALSE
5. Scattered believers who are persecuted can also be compared to <u>fire embers</u> or <u>starfish</u> because of the multiplying effect they have.

NOTES

NOTES

NOTES

NOTES